BRONSON
INSIDE AND OUT

MIRROR BOOKS

© Julie Shaw

The rights of Julie Shaw to be identified as the author of this book have been asserted, in accordance with the Copyright, Designs and Patents Act 1988.

1

Published in Great Britain and Ireland in 2025 by Mirror Books, a Reach PLC business.

Photographic Acknowledgements:
Alamy, Charles Salvador and Irene Dunroe Personal Collection, Mirrorpix

www.mirrorbooks.co.uk
@TheMirrorBooks

Print ISBN 9781917439176
eBook ISBN 9781917439183

Editing and Production: Jo Sollis, Christine Costello
Cover Design: Chris Collins

Printed and bound in Great Britain by
CPI Group (UK) Ltd, Croydon, CR0 4YY

BRONSON
INSIDE AND OUT

**IRENE DUNROE, CHARLES BRONSON
AND JULIE SHAW**

MIRROR BOOKS

I'd like to dedicate this book to our son, Michael Peterson, who has travelled this roller coaster of a journey with both me and his dad, every step of the way. Also to my beautiful mum, because without her by our sides, we would never have made it. I bless them both, every day.

– IRENE DUNROE

I dedicate this book to my Irene. The strongest woman I've ever known! To all the great friends I've made in my many years behind bars - sadly, most have now passed, but the memories! Those memories will live with me until the day I die.

And to my son, Michael, hang fire, son, you and your dad will share a pint one day soon, I can feel it! Finally, a special thanks to my many, many supporters out there, who find it in their hearts to write to me, or to join social media groups to remember me and chat about me, I promise you, I appreciate it more than you could ever know. Thank you.

I'd also like to dedicate this to my brother, Mark Peterson, who was buried on my birthday, 6/12/2024, love and respect, brother, always in my heart, Micky x

– CHARLES BRONSON

I dedicate this story to all those left behind. The wives, husbands, children and parents who find themselves bereft when their loved one gets locked away for years. You are often the forgotten ones, the ones having to pick up all the pieces, keep the family together, and find a way to get up each day and move forward.

Life might be harsh for the one in prison, but you never asked for the prison you now find yourself in, it was forced upon you, and now, life as you knew it has stopped and you find yourself lost. I send you my love and best wishes for the future, you are stronger than you think!

– JULIE SHAW

INTRODUCTION

BY JULIE SHAW

LAST YEAR I was approached online by Irene Dunroe and her daughter, Leicia. Having already written a series of true crime books, they were familiar with my work and reached out. I was surprised to be asked if I'd like to write Irene's story, which sounded so interesting that I immediately agreed. However, as we got into the writing process, it became clear to me that Irene still had very strong feelings about Mick and was still in touch with him regularly. Mick, who is now known as Charles Salvador – or Charles Bronson by some – was born Michael Peterson. He has changed his name twice by deed poll. Despite this, his ex-wife Irene will forever refer to him as her Mick. In our early discussions about the book, I suggested to her that this story was as much his as it was hers, and that perhaps Mick might want to be involved.

Two weeks later, I received a long letter from him, which

ended with him saying that he'd love to be involved and he would be happy to help in any way he could. From then on, the story we were telling began to take a different turn…

I studied both Psychology and Criminology at university, and have always worked in those fields, so I immediately recognised that there was a lot more to both Irene and Mick than the general public know, and I really wanted to explore that. I learned, through many letters from Mick, that lots of things happening on the outside of prison had a direct effect on the way he behaved inside, and I wanted to make that clear to readers. With this in mind, throughout the narrative, you'll see a selection of reports written by me to try and explain what I thought was going on at the time of the previous chapters. I hope this doesn't detract from your reading experience, and they can be skipped if you wish, but you may find them useful or interesting.

Charles Salvador is currently preparing for his next parole hearing. Below is a summary of the findings of his last hearing in 2023.

The narrative is constructed based on many hours of talking with both Irene and Charles and also lots of handwritten letters and emails sent from the prison where Charles is currently serving. Irene had been keeping detailed notes for years, and had in fact started writing her own book. She very kindly sent me everything she had written down, so I was able to take lots of material directly from that. I also spent many hours researching newspaper stories and newsreels that helped me gain further insight into Charles in his younger years.

PROLOGUE

BY CHARLES SALVADOR

I'M SO happy that this book has finally come to fruition.

As you all know, I've had lots of time to think over the years, although looking back, I don't think I'd have done anything any differently, I can admit that part of my anger came from what I had left behind, outside of these prison walls.

It's not just your liberty that you lose, it's everything else. For me that was my wife and my boy, and much as I tried to put thoughts of loss to one side, I just couldn't. I had to let Irene go, for her sanity, because I knew if our being apart was driving me fucking mad then it would be just the same for her, and I couldn't do that, not to my Irene.

Helping write this book has made me think a lot about the past, how much the system has changed and – fuck me! – how much I've changed! Has the system changed me? Are we actually all just a product of our environ-ment? I'll let you decide that as you read.

As I write, I'm preparing for my jam roll (parole hearing) and I'm really hoping that this time, enough is enough. I've done my time. Fucking hell, I believe I've done years more than my time! I have a huge network of friends and supporters, I have my art, which sells regularly and can offer me a secure income on the outside and, despite it all, I have my sanity. I'm all set to enjoy what is left of my life, to reconnect with my loved ones and especially my son, Michael. My freedom is just a heartbeat away, I can feel it!

Charles Salvador
Adios Amigos!

SUMMARY OF THE PAROLE BOARD DECISION

HEARING VIA VIDEO LINK
MARCH 10, 2023

NAME: CHARLES SALVADOR

Mr Salvador has been in his current prison since 2019. He is held in secure conditions which he feels are better than those he has experienced in the past and that he is treated with kindness. The panel noted that there had been a prolonged period of improved behaviour and that Mr Salvador had been working with professionals. He has been engaging with specialist work with a psychologist, although Mr Salvador told the panel that he had not learnt much from the sessions.

Due to staff shortages, Mr Salvador spends 23 hours a day in his cell and chooses to spend the time out of his cell in the gym or the exercise yard. Typically, he will speak to other prisoners in his association group for about 10 minutes a day. He is allowed to associate with three prisoners and dislikes one of them. He has told the prisoner that he dislikes that he will not be talking to him and they co-exist without bothering each other. The panel considered the limited time out of his cell has offered little opportunity for Mr Salvador's ability to manage himself in conflict situations to be tested.

The panel noted that Mr Salvador lives by his own rules and code of conduct and that he judges others to his own standards. Set against this, there has been evidence of Mr Salvador breaking prison rules which he considered to be 'petty' and 'minor' and that get in the way of him achieving his aims and doing what he wants to do. There have also been a number of occasional verbal outbursts reported. The panel consider Mr Salvador to have unrealistic expectations of others and this, combined with his breaching of prison rules, suggests that he would be unlikely to comply with any risk management strategies that could be put in place. In the panel's view, Mr Salvador's ability to manage himself safely in a less controlled environment where his expectations are challenged, or are not met, is yet to be tested.

Most witnesses at the oral hearing did not recommend Mr Salvador's release or his progression to an open prison. The panel was told that the current sentence plan was for Mr Salvador to move to another prison where he can show how he manages himself in a more open unit with fewer restrictions on his behaviour.

The psychologist assigned by Mr Salvador's legal representative had not recommended release in her written report. In her evidence at the oral hearing, the psychologist's view fluctuated while she was questioned, ranging from progression in a closed prison, progression to an open prison to potential release. Her final preference was for Mr Salvador to be moved to an open prison.

In this case, factors which would reduce the risk of re-offending were identified as Mr Salvador's sense of hope for the future and his commitment to progression. The panel noted that he has realistic long-term goals that are providing him with a focus. His artwork is now a central part of his life that was not previously present when he was offending in the community. This has increased his self-esteem and provides a potential opportunity for him to secure a legitimate income to fund his lifestyle upon release.

The panel examined the release plan provided by Mr Salvador's probation officer and weighed its proposals against the risks they had assessed. The plan included a requirement to reside in designated accommodation, as well as strict limitations on Mr Salvador's contacts, movements and activities. Mr Salvador also set out his own plans for the future.

The panel concluded the release plan would be robust because it would provide a strict set of external controls. However, the panel was concerned that Mr Salvador had not yet developed the necessary internal controls that he could use to safely manage his risk of future violence. The panel determined that in the absence of those internal controls, the external controls of the risk management plan would be unlikely to be sufficient to manage Mr Salvador's level of risk.

The panel noted that he is presently in a highly restricted environment and his general attitude towards compliance is yet to be tested in conditions of less security. Consequently, the panel did not consider the release plan to be sufficient at this stage in managing Mr Salvador safely in the community.

Decision: No direction for release on parole licence and no recommendation for transfer to an open prison.

After considering the circumstances of his offending, the progress that Mr Salvador has made while in custody and the evidence presented at the hearings, the panel was not satisfied that Mr Salvador was suitable for release. Nor did the panel recommend to the Secretary of State that he should be transferred to an open prison.

The panel noted that Mr Salvador has spent most of the last 48 years in custody and that much of this time has been in conditions of segregation. The panel accepted that Mr Salvador genuinely wants to progress and that he is motivated to work towards his release. It was thought that there was evidence of improved self-control and better emotional management.

However, the panel was mindful of his history of persistent rule breaking and that Mr Salvador sees little wrong with this. He lives his life rigidly by his own rules and code of conduct and is quick to judge others by his own standards. His positive progress has to be assessed in the context of him being held in a highly restrictive environment. In the panel's view, it is unknown exactly what is containing Mr Salvador's risk. It is unclear whether the strong external controls of custody are mainly responsible or whether his attitudes have genuinely changed.

The panel could not be satisfied that Mr Salvador has the skills to manage his risk of future violence until he has been extensively tested outside of his current highly restricted environment. The movement and categorisation of prisoners are entirely a matter for the Secretary of State, and parole panels will not ordinarily comment on such matters. However in this particular circumstances, the panel observed that there is an identified pathway for Salvador in custody and the evidence supported such a move within a closed prison.

In the panel's view, this is a pivotal point in Mr Salvador's sentence when his motivation to desist from violence is at its highest. Both psychologists instructed by Mr Salvador's legal representative were unequivocal in their view that he no longer requires secure placement in his current prison.

He will be eligible for another parole review in due course.

CHAPTER ONE

IRENE

'KELSEY!' MR Dunbar yelled, his booming voice shocking me back to reality. 'Irene Kelsey, is there something very interesting outside that window, and is it related to fractions?'

'No sir,' I answered quietly as I turned back to the teacher and tried to concentrate on the scrawling gobbledegook on the blackboard. Anything was infinitely more interesting than maths I thought, as my mind wandered again. I hated it and simply could not for the life of me see the point. When was I ever going to need to know about bloody Pythagoras, I thought. I enjoyed most other subjects and didn't mind learning as a rule, perhaps it was just Mr Dunbar that I didn't like. Regardless, I was a dreamer, and I much preferred being outside in the fresh air, hence the lure of the windows when I was trapped inside a classroom. I couldn't wait to leave school.

By any standards, my young life was idyllic, living in a huge house with sprawling grounds in the suburbs of The Wirral. The neighbours and any visitors always assumed we were either famous for something or other, or super rich. My parents, Ivy and Archibald, were quite private people so this only added to the mystery, and they would smile when the whispers started up each time my Dad bought a new boat, which he either moored in Anglesey on the Menai Strait or kept stacked by our garage while he worked on them. He actually built a couple of cabin cruisers too, and he absolutely loved his sea fishing. Not me though, despite him trying to get me interested in his hobbies. I hated the water and the wellington boots he wanted me to wear, and was far more interested in the huge quarry that was right by our house.

I was born in 1952, the youngest of four siblings, and was always known as 'the babbi'. My Dad always called me this even when I was a grown adult! The huge quarry I was so attracted to has long since gone, but as a child I would beg my brother, Rob, to take me up there with him to watch all the men on their motorbikes. They were defying death in my eyes, as they raced up and down the sides of the enormous quarry. It was so exciting to watch as they roared around and did stunts, even the smell of the petrol was exciting to me. I loved everything about it. Out there I felt such a sense of freedom and I think I always knew that I would eventually break away from the confines of my comfortable life. My Dad was ex-military and he liked things to be just so. He had big expectations of all of his children, but the pull of something more meant that I was destined to go my own way. There was another, more thrilling path for me, and although I didn't know it at the time, my refusal to conform and accept the easy life were simply steps along that path.

My Dad had five brothers and a younger sister, and they had all been brought up on a big working farm. After my Grandad died, two of Dad's brothers, Uncle Charlie and Uncle Ernie, took over the running of it. Of course, I loved going there to visit. I played with the pigs as often as I could. There were geese too and they would always end up chasing my brother Rod, which was hysterical.

My uncle Ernie, a gunsmith by trade, was known as an eccentric, but I just thought he was funny. He would tell stories about how he used to sell his guns to people from all over the world, the toffs, as my Dad would say. Apparently, he once sold a gun to Sean Connery! I've never known if that was in fact true, or just my uncle telling one of his tall tales, but it was a great story to tell. The guns were for clay pigeon shooting when the rich and famous went for days out in the country estates, and each gun was worth a small fortune. Uncle Ernie had them all carefully lined up along the walls of his shed on the farm. He loved his guns so much that he eventually ended up moving into his shed and sleeping alongside them. No wonder the locals called him eccentric. You would think that my Dad, having come from such a family, would have a more relaxed attitude with his children, but he didn't, and we all feared his wrath.

My older sisters, Janet and Pauline, feared him too, even though they were practically grown-ups, dating wealthy young men that they intended to marry.

'Stand there and keep watch,' Janet would often say to me, as she plonked me a few feet away from her and her boyfriend.

'If you see or hear our Dad come out, let me know as quick as you can, you got that, Irene?'

I nodded and grinned as she walked a little further down the lane to canoodle with her fellow, then I'd turn and watch intently for any signs of the enemy, who would for sure be stalking the lane at bang on nine o'clock.

'She's still not bloody back, Ivy!' he would shout towards the house as he pointed at his wristwatch. 'He'll be knocking about with that bloody cowboy from the village, just wait till she gets home, she's going to know about it.'

'Oh, come inside, dear,' Mum would say, trying to soothe him before the inevitable argument when my poor sister got in. 'You'll catch your death out here, and besides, she's only one minute late, it'll be those new heels she was wearing, it's murder trying to walk fast in those.'

Poor Mum tried her best, always, to keep the peace in our home. She agreed with my siblings that 9.00pm was far too early for grown adults to have to be home, but at the same time she said we all had to accept that rules were rules and, despite that being a stupid rule, Dad was the head of the house, and as such, had to be obeyed. That stood for Mum too, she very rarely got a say in any decisions Dad made.

I learnt a lot by observing Janet, Pauline and Rodney. By the time I was about 14 it occurred to me that wealth and privilege didn't necessarily equate to a happy life – which all my school friends assumed. I learned that a lot of rules were pointless and only seemed to be in place so that someone higher in the pecking order could wield control and, most importantly, that I could never really become the young lady my Dad wanted me to be. There would be no grammar school for me, no posh finishing school either, and definitely no marrying me off to some rich boy. I decided right back then that I wanted to work, to fend for myself and to experience lots of friendships with exciting people. I loved my parents dearly, but as soon as I mentally removed the burden of their high expectations I became a much happier girl.

By 1966 I was well into the music and fashion scene, and would spend every penny I had on the wonderful clothes I loved. Clothes that were not necessarily considered trendy by my peers, but ones which I knew looked good on me.

'Come on, Irene,' my best friend Lynne would shout as she waited by the bus stop for me. 'Can't keep the shops waiting.'

'I'm worth the wait,' I shouted back, laughing as I tried to avoid kicking up any dirt that might stain my new, pristine white trousers that I was wearing, along with a tailored Ben Sherman checked shirt. 'Where is it today?' I asked as I joined her, 'Liverpool or Birkenhead?'

'Liverpool,' Lynne said, 'I want to go to that new Chelsea Girl that's opened, I want a new mini dress to wear for Sunday.'

I giggled. We loved our Saturday shopping days in the town centres, but Sundays were the best. On Sundays we would dress up in all our new purchases, make up our faces and do our hair, and then hop on the bus to Parkgate, a lovely seaside area with a long promenade. After sitting in our favourite cafe, having tea and crumpets, we would then stroll arm in arm up and down the parade, while boys and hunky guys would slowly drive by us in their posh cars, beeping their horns at us. It was wonderful, it was thrilling, it was everything my parents hated about how the 1960s were shaping up. Of course, if they hated it, I loved it.

'Join the tennis club at Parkgate,' my Dad would plead. 'Both your sisters did, and you will meet a nice young man there, one with status and the money to take care of you, Irene.'

'I don't like tennis,' I reasoned, 'and I don't want to meet a nice young man either, thank you very much, I'm happy with my friends.' I put my hand on Dad's arm as

I saw his crestfallen look. 'Don't worry about me, Dad,' I said. 'I've promised Mum I'm staying on at school to get my typing exams and I'll get a job. I'm going to be just fine.'

He did worry about me though. After all, I was 'the babbi', and my brother Rod, despite being classed as a man now at 19, was still coming home drunk on occasions and gambling now and again. And if my own brother was an example of what guys of that age were generally like, no wonder Dad was worried! I would often have to block my ears with my pillow as I lay in bed so I couldn't hear the angry arguments that would be going on downstairs when poor Rodney didn't make it home in time, yet again. I remember going down to the kitchen one morning after such an argument and I was surprised to see there was money scattered all over the floor with my mother knelt down, scooping it up.

'Where's all this from, Mum?' I asked as I knelt beside her to help her pick up £10 and £20 notes.

'It's Rodney's,' she whispered, her face looking drawn. 'He won it at Chester races apparently. Your Dad wasn't happy about it. You know how he is about gambling, Irene.'

'I heard.' I said, giving her a look that said I understood. We finished picking it all up in silence. As I stacked it on the dresser, Mum stood up and smiled at me.

'Cup of tea, love?' She asked brightly.

I knew the routine by now. Put the bad stuff to one side and smile. Oh, and a nice cup of tea solved everything.

'Ooh! Lovely,' I said. 'I'm parched.'

Mum set to work on our morning cuppa while I, I'm ashamed to say, quickly stuffed one of my brother's £10 notes into my dressing gown pocket. That tenner was swiftly spent on two beautiful mini, shift dresses from Miss Selfridge's in Liverpool. I thought I looked stunning the following Sunday, strutting down that parade in my proceeds of crime, a pale green, Grecian-style mini dress.

I was growing up fast, and embracing the late 60s and all it had to offer, so I needed a decent job in order to fund my lifestyle. My friends and I had now entered the world of clubbing, and boy did we love it! The music, the dancing, the boys, it was all so thrilling, and the nightlife was teeming with young people just like me, out for a laugh and to have fun. Honestly, I truly believe I could have had a different boyfriend every single night of the week if I'd wanted, but really, I was happiest with my girlfriends, dancing the night away and ogling the hunks from a safe distance. Sometimes I'd get chatting with a boy I fancied, and sometimes I'd allow him to walk me home, but usually it was out of necessity – if I'd spent my taxi fare or wanted him to buy me a drink or two. It was all very innocent back in those days.

Eventually, I did get a decent job after staying on at school as I'd promised, as an audio typist at Littlewoods

Pools. My mother accompanied me to the interview and as soon as we entered the reception area, I smiled as I heard the piped pop music playing in the background.

'Oh, I suppose you'll love it here,' my mother said, rolling her eyes. 'All this ridiculous music blaring out.'

The music of course was an enticing plus for me, but the reality was that I wanted this job badly. That nagging pull that I was becoming accustomed to was creeping up on me again, and I just knew that getting this job was the key to opening up a whole new chapter of my life. Typing all day wasn't everybody's idea of an exciting job, and although I had a headful of dreams, deep down, I knew it wouldn't be that fulfilling, but it was a means to an end. As a young woman who wanted to experience a fun life, I had to earn a decent wage. I had to work hard and pay my way.

I got the job immediately and, suddenly, the world was my oyster. Or so it seemed.

CHAPTER TWO

MICK

I RECKON they've argued about nature v nurture since time began. They've argued about it, but they've never settled on it, have they? See, it's all a load of old bollocks, really. I mean, I can see how the argument for 'you are what eat' pans out; you eat shit, you get fat and unhealthy, that's simple, but as for 'are you born bad – or good for that matter – or are you a product of your environment', well that's not an easy answer is it? See, I was born good. Anyone will tell you that. My Mum and Dad, Eira and Joe Peterson ran the local Conservative club in Aberystwyth, a lovely little seaside town, and life was great for me. I was taught good manners, to respect ladies and to be a good boy for my parents.

I was born Michael Gordon Peterson in 1952 in Luton, but we moved to the club when I was still a baby. When I was four though, we moved back to Luton, back to the hustle and bustle of a big town. I had a big brother, John, so school was never a problem for me really and, to be honest, I was a big lad for my age so I didn't get messed with. We were also very well respected, in part because my aunt and uncle were both mayors of the town while I was young. We were just a nice, average, hardworking, close family. I tried my hardest to be good at school because that's what my parents wanted for me, but you know what I couldn't stand? Bullies! I hated them with a passion and I couldn't stand it if I saw some unfortunate getting picked on, or being battered by some bigger kid. I couldn't help myself but charge in and sort the big bastards out.

'Not again, Micky!' My Mum would say as she dragged me up from the bench outside the headmaster's office after she'd been called into school for the umpteenth time because of my fighting. 'Honestly, I'm getting fed up with this. Now, sort your jumper out and stand up straight. I'm warning you, Micky, not a word when we step inside that office, you hear?'

I'd nod meekly, genuinely sorry that she'd had to leave work early to come collect me. I wouldn't mind but it wasn't even my fault, I'd only been sticking up for some poor boy who had been getting his head kicked in. His crime? Having a snotty nose, can you believe it? I followed mum into the office and bowed my head as the teacher sternly told my mother, 'Mrs Peterson, I'm afraid it's about fighting again, and this time the lad on the other end of his fist ended up with a bloody nose and a missing tooth. I've had all on, talking Mrs Tolan out of calling the Bobbies.' My teacher shrugged his shoulders and I saw him point at me and said, 'So you see, his behaviour is getting worse, and…'

'Can I just say,' my mother interrupted, 'before you start talking about expelling him again, like I told you before, my Micky is a good boy, and yes, he's a big lad and can look after himself, but that Billy Tolan is a bully, he must have done something – that I can promise you!'

I chanced raising my head, 'He did, Mum, he…'

'Not a word, I said, Micky, not a word.' Mum said, giving me her warning look and her pointy finger.

'Be that as it may, Mrs Peterson,' the teacher said after a long sigh, 'we can't have this carry on every week. One more incident and I'm afraid he's gone. My hands are tied.'

'I'm very grateful,' my Mum said, 'and his Dad and me, we'll have another chat with Micky this evening. This'll be the end of it, you'll see.'

With that she grabbed me by the hand and practically dragged me all the way home. I wouldn't have dared to start with her, but I was angry inside. I mean, where's the justice in that? I didn't even really know the little snotty kid that got the hiding, but it was clear he couldn't ever have a brawl, he was tiny! And it wasn't his fault he had a snotty nose all the time and never had a handkerchief.

They all took the piss out of him, called him Greensleeves – like the song we once sang in assembly, on account of him wiping his nose on his school jumper sleeve all the time. Poor kid never stood a chance against Billy Tolan and I wasn't going to wear that. I couldn't fathom why nobody understood that.

Truth be told, although I was never going to be a bully, I did enjoy a scrap. It made me feel quite relaxed afterwards, but only if the one I scrapped with deserved it. If I ever got into it with somebody who was in the right, then I felt bad afterwards, and angry with myself.

I never got into much bother with my parents though, even after a fight at school or with one of the kids in the neighbourhood – I think they understood me. They would sit me down and try to make me see that beating someone up was only ever going to get me into trouble, but they did acknowledge that I only really went after the bad kids and the bullies. They would tell me it wasn't up to me to sort them out. But if not me, then who? They had to have done something in front of me for me to react in the first place, no parents or teachers or coppers were around when they did whatever they did, and I seemed to be the only one around who would confront them. I really didn't see how I was in the wrong.

Not long after that incident at school, my mum announced she was going to have another baby, and me and my older brother John were both going to be big brothers. John was practically a grown up by now and wasn't really that bothered, but I was excited, and really hoped it would be a boy who I could protect and teach stuff to. I was over the moon when she had little baby Mark. He was tiny and the whole family loved him dearly. I think it was after Mark was born that my parents first started talking about moving closer to my nan and grandad. They reckoned it would be good for me to have a fresh start in a new school, and there was plenty of work up there apparently for my dad, who had trained as a painter and decorator. So, when my little brother was still a toddler, we made our big family move to a village near Ellesmere Port in Cheshire, near my nan's house.

We were a very close family, and once we'd settled, my dad taught me how to play cards so I could join him, grandad and my uncle once a week for a boys' night where we'd all play cards for matchsticks. I loved those nights.

I started to make friends fast. I was the new kid on the block with a Cockney accent to boot, so I think they all found me interesting. My size, however, meant that it was older kids that wanted to be mates with me, and it was either my gob or my demeanour, but they somehow knew I could have a brawl – and win. It wasn't long before I was hanging around with three or four of the local bad boys. Not because I sought them out, I didn't know anybody up there. I guess I just attracted them somehow. Anyway, soon enough we were a gang.

The lads were petty thieves and general trouble causers and, with the lack of anything else more exciting to do, I jumped on their bandwagon. Now, remember, my family weren't short of a bob or two. I could have anything I wanted, I never went short. But there we were, out robbing the local shops for sweets, ciggies, magazines, anything really. We'd be straight in and out, often having customers and the shopkeeper chasing us down the street, and we'd be laughing our heads off. I wasn't well known around the area at the time, so I never had the locals knocking at our door to complain, it was all good at the start.

I was having a fair few fights in my new school too, usually with kids who'd heard I was part of a gang and they were wanting to make a name for themselves. Part of me wanted to really batter them when they pissed me off, but a little voice in my head always stopped me from going too far. I didn't want to upset Mum, who now had a job in a nice hotel, and my Dad, who was out working all the time. I didn't want them having to be dragged into school on the daily. So I started wagging off, to avoid temptation. I don't think school really cared if I wasn't there, I think it gave them a bit of a break if I'm honest. It didn't occur to me at the time, but the little gang, the robbing, the fighting, meant I was allowing crime to become part of my life, and I went from corner shops to bikes, then to cars and criminal damage. It wasn't long before I had my first brush with the law. I ended up in court and got a severe reprimand.

It didn't stop me, I just became better at evading capture. I was growing up fast. I was big, strong and mean when I had to be, but I still cared. I loved my family and never ever wanted to hurt or disappoint my parents who loved me. They were dead proud after I left school and got a job on a local building site, hod carrying, and they smiled with pride as I spent my wages on nice suits and shirts and ties for my nights out on the town with my friends.

'You look ever so smart, Micky,' my Mum would say as she watched me getting done up. 'Not like the yobs you see these days, a proper gent, you are. Let me give you a couple of quid, son, for a few drinks, you might meet a lovely girl down there, you never know.'

I smiled through the mirror as I straightened my tie.

'You keep your money, Mum,' I said. 'I got plenty, and it'd have to be some woman for me – she'd have to live up to you Mum.'

I meant it, too. My Mum was a proper lady. Little did she know I'd already been introduced to some of the local girls already, but they didn't really mean anything to me. A man has his needs and all, but the 'lovely girl' my mother wanted for me didn't exist in the company I was keeping. Not yet anyway.

CHAPTER THREE

IRENE

BY THE age of 17, I felt I'd finally got a routine going in my life, one that I was happy with. I had my friends, a steady job, good money, a fabulous wardrobe filled with all the best clothes and a very busy social life. I'd had lots of dates with local boys, but because of my penchant for thrill seeking, I always tended to go for the 'bad boys', much to my parent's horror. One had been in borstal, another stole cars, others were simply considered wasters, but I couldn't help it, I was like a magnet to them! It wasn't that I was into crime in any way, I had high morals and had been brought up to understand that one had to work to earn one's money. It was more that I always had this stomach-knotting urge to push boundaries, I think, and I was never satisfied with the mundane.

I loved my nights out. I could go out clubbing even on weekdays and still get myself up and ready for work the next day. So it wasn't out of the ordinary when my friend, Linda, called me one Wednesday night, raving about a band that were appearing in Great Sutton.

'Oh, say you'll come with me, Irene,' she pleaded. 'I've been wanting to see these for months and they're on at The Bull, pretty please!'

I laughed.

'You don't have to ask me twice,' I said. 'What are you wearing?'

'I've got a new yellow mini dress,' she said. 'I thought I'd wear that and my slingbacks, what about you?'

'My Mum bought me those new white boots I've been wanting,' I said. 'I'm going to put my white dress on and wear those.'

I felt fabulous in my new outfit, and I'd even found a white headband to hold back my long, dark hair. I could feel the bristle of excitement as we found a table to sit at while waiting for the band to start.

'See those guys that have just walked in,' Linda shouted above the din. 'That one in the suit is staring over at you, Irene, flash him a smile, mate, we might get a free drink.'

We both laughed but I stole a glance in the direction Linda had indicated and I was immediately interested – in one of them at least. He looked like a proper man in his tailored cream suit with a handkerchief in his top pocket and an open necked shirt on. I couldn't stop staring, he was gorgeous! So handsome, with a little Mexican moustache and long sideburns, he just commanded attention.

'Oh my god, Linda, don't look up, they're coming over,' I said, frantically turning my head so it didn't look like I was watching them.

Linda giggled as they approached the table and introduced themselves as Mick and John.

'I'm Linda,' she said, fluttering her eyelashes at the one called John, 'and this is my friend, Irene. Join us if you like, there's a brilliant band coming on.'

Mick was even more handsome close up and, as he smiled at me, I felt like I could see into his very soul through his deep brown eyes. I could barely breathe. I knew, right there in that moment, that this was what being in love felt like. I was smitten.

The rest of that evening was just the best – drinking Cherry B and cider, dancing and singing along to the band, chatting and laughing. I felt like I had finally found what I'd been searching for. Mick, with his funny Cockney accent and his perfect manners, made me feel more at ease than I'd ever felt in my life. I'd only just met the man, but I felt I'd been looking for him forever. He drove us all home at the end of the evening and we shared a lovely snog before exchanging numbers and arranging to meet up again in a couple of nights. I was walking on air as I practically skipped up our drive. I barely slept that night as I replayed every moment in my head. How he'd opened the car door for me to get in, then leapt out when we stopped and ran around the car to open my door again so he could take my hand and help me out. I couldn't wait for our next date.

I didn't have to wait long. It was the Friday, in fact, when Mick phoned.

'How are you doing, Princess?' Mick asked. 'I had a lovely night on Wednesday, but I can't wait to see you again. You up for a date tonight?'

'I had a lovely night too,' I said, suddenly feeling shy, 'and yes, I'd love to go out tonight. Will your friend be there too? Only, I could ask Linda along, I think she liked him.'

Mick laughed softly down the phone.

'That was going to be my next suggestion,' he said. 'Because John liked your friend too. We're going to take you to The Waverley, it's in Ellesmere Port, have you been before?'

'No, but I've heard it's a good place for dancing,' I said. 'I'll look forward to it.'

'Good girl,' Mick said. 'We'll pick you both up at 7.00pm, from the end of your drive?'

'Yes,' I said, cringing a little. It seemed silly at my age having to be picked up on the lane rather than from outside the door, but I couldn't be bothered with all the questions I'd get from Mum and Dad. Best they assumed I was just out with Linda for now.

Once again, I had the best night. This time Mick wore a pale brown suit with a cream, open necked shirt. He was by far the most handsome man in the club and I felt so proud to be by his side, especially when he took to the dance-floor by himself! I had rarely seen a man dance alone, but Mick was brilliant. He got down on the floor, supported by one hand, and just threw the most amazing moves I'd ever seen. A huge circle of people formed around him, clapping and cheering as he entertained everybody. It was as if he were lost in the music.

'Wow!' I said as he walked across the dancefloor and took my hand. 'You certainly know how to put on a show. That was brilliant, Mick.'

He winked at me and smiled.

'All for you, baby,' he said as he spun me around and took me in his arms. 'You make me want to dance every time I see this beautiful face.' He kissed me, not a bit bothered that everyone was watching us.

I don't know how I knew this, and I'd never been to that club before, but I had the feeling that everybody in there knew Mick. Nobody bothered us, or even spoke to us, but it was like we were being treated like celebrities or something. People would part a pathway through the crowd if I got up to use the ladies' room, and the same when Mick stood up to go to the bar, it was odd but nice. Drinks would appear on our table from random strangers and, despite the club being packed to the rafters, it was like our little table had a protective bubble around it that nobody else would enter. It was weird, but I soon got used to it.

We started going out regularly and it wasn't long before I began to realise that everybody in our orbit did indeed know Mick. After a night out we usually ended up going for a meal to Mick's favourite Chinese restaurant. It was near the docks in quite a rough area of Ellesmere Port, but the food there was divine so I could see why it was so popular. The only problem I could see was that the restaurant was attached to a pub that was as rough as the area it was in. It was a late-night bar, which meant that every drunk in Ellesmere Port ended up there, or so it seemed. It also meant that quite a lot of fights broke out, which in turn meant that I was about to be educated on the other side of my beautifully mannered boyfriend…

One night, I was barely through my second course of our Chinese banquet, when two men dressed in suits approached our table.

'Need a quick word, Micky,' the taller one of the men said, with a sense of urgency.

Mick didn't bat an eyelid at either of them, but he placed down his fork and reached across the table to put his hands on mine. He smiled tenderly at me before asking, 'Are you almost done there, Princess?'

I glanced at the men, wondering what was going on, then back at Mick. 'Um, yes, I think so,' I said before staring longingly at the lovely food I was sure I'd have to leave. 'Do we need to go now or something?'

Mick smiled again and then signalled for a waiter. 'Taxi please,' he said, 'for my young lady, and make it quick if you don't mind.'

I later learned through Linda that Mick was known as a sort of trouble shooter. When fights broke out in the pub next door, someone would get word to Mick and he'd immediately go sort it out. By all accounts he quite enjoyed it and would always, always take the side of the underdog and ensure that the fight was as fair as possible. Rather than be shocked at this revelation, I felt quite proud. Mick really was my knight in shining armour and I'd never felt so safe in my whole life.

I quickly got used to nights like this, my Mick being called upon to get involved with some brawl, but I never got used to having to leave platefuls of delicious food. That, in my opinion, was criminal. It happened regularly though and off I'd go, escorted into a taxi for my own safety, my hero waving me off with a huge smile on his lovely face. It was almost enough to make up for leaving a half-eaten meal – almost! I simply learned how to eat very quickly.

CHAPTER FOUR

MICK

AFTER LEAVING school, I knew I'd have to start making my own way in the world, specifically earning some money so that I could start to enjoy my life as an adult.

I had quite the reputation going on in both Ellesmere Port and my home town of Luton and was fast becoming known as the go-to fellow for sorting out a spot of bother. I was very strong, very fast, and I could take down an opponent in seconds if I needed to. On other occasions though, a different service was required, one that wasn't so fast and would require a long-term technique involving intimidation and basically putting the fear of god into people. Either way was fine by me, I was paid good money and, as I said before, I quite enjoyed getting into a ruck. It was like letting off steam for me and it got the boredom out of my system temporarily.

That was part of my problem, see I was very easily bored

and always searching for an adrenaline rush. I'd had lots of different jobs on the building sites because manual labour gave me that same energy release I needed. But just like at school, if I saw any man taking the piss out of another who didn't deserve it, I'd see red and automatically jump in to give the bully a pasting. You'd think adult men would grow out of bullying, wouldn't you? Sadly, they didn't. I liked to observe people from a young age and learned to read their demeanours. I often liked to watch a situation unravel and try to predict what would happen next. I suppose this was in part due to boredom too, but I was really surprised to learn, over and over again, that most men fell into one of two camps. They were either kind, compassionate, stand-up guys, or they were weak, nasty creatures, lacking in something so basic that they would hurt others just to feel better about themselves.

So, whether it be on the building sites, in the factories or on the markets, there was always some nasty bastard I'd have to smack in the face that would cause me to lose my job. I didn't always get the sack. Sometimes I'd just walk away and tell them to stuff it before I did any real damage.

I knew my limits and I certainly didn't want anyone to think I was one of the bullies, so I'd make my point and then leave the job. Of course, word got around, like it does, and pretty soon I'd have the local dodgy dealers sending word out that they had an earner for me. It might involve collecting debts from some silly geezer who was refusing to pay a large sum of money back after a loan, or often it would be to go teach someone a lesson – always a bad man. Then, sometimes, it was just to accompany a couple of guys to a meeting. I was there in these instances as a back-up, just in case the meet went tits up. I was always suited and booted, which I think surprised some people, but I'd been brought up to always look smart, always be a gentleman, and I was. It was fucking annoying when I got blood on a new suit or shirt though, but I had to take the lows with the highs, didn't I?

It was always nice to go out for a few drinks after a hard day's graft, so when I met up with one of my best mates one Wednesday in a small boozer I'd had a bit of business in, I was happy when he suggested we go and let off a bit of steam.

'I thought we'd go to The Bull in Sutton,' John said. 'They have bands on, a bit of dancing, lots of lovely birds, come on, what do you say?'

I knew The Bull, I'd been in a few times.

'You twisted my arm, mate,' I said as I downed my first pint. 'We'll take my car though, I can't leave it round here, they'll have my fucking wheels off before the morning.'

John laughed.

'You been upsetting the locals, Micky?' he asked. 'Come on, mate, let's nash.'

He grabbed his coat and followed me out of the door.

'Only one local, John,' I said as I straightened my tie

and grinned before jumping into the driver's seat, 'and trust me, it wouldn't be him who'd touch my car, that would require having the use of your fingers, mate.'

The minute we walked through the doors at The Bull, I spotted her. The most beautiful girl I'd ever seen in my life. I felt like I'd been punched in the throat and could hardly breathe. I didn't know what the fuck had hit me and I'd never felt anything like it in my life before, but I could not tear my eyes away from her. I couldn't even get a word out to John, I just followed him to the bar trying to regulate my breathing while trying to steal a look at that girl. She was sitting next to another girl, but it was only the one in white I was interested in. I took in everything about her all at once, the white, zip-up boots, the short white dress and the long, glossy black hair. *She's an angel*, I thought, and for the first time I can remember, I felt like crying, it was madness.

'Here you go, mate,' John said, handing me a pint and then grinning. 'I see you've clocked the same birds as me then. That one in white can't take her fucking eyes off you, Micky, do you wanna go over, introduce ourselves like?'

I don't know what it was, but it was something about John using bad language while speaking about that vision in white, it made me prickle, it just didn't seem right.

'Yes, let's,' I said. 'But, John, no swearing, they're not your usual type, they're young ladies, I can just tell.'

'Got it, boss.' John said, as he grinned and made his way over to their table.

Thankfully, John and the girl called Linda hit it off straight away, leaving me to get to know Irene. My first impressions had been spot on, she was unlike any other girl I'd ever met. Softly spoken with impeccable manners, I could tell immediately that she'd had a good upbringing. Right from the get-go, I knew I wanted to protect her from this world and anything bad in it. I could have listened to her all night and, although she kept getting up for a dance, and I'd join her, all I really wanted to do was sit down with her and just watch her smile. She was funny too, and I actually got a jaw ache from laughing when she cracked a joke with her friend, Linda. It was a truly magical night that I never wanted to end.

'I've really enjoyed myself, Mick,' Irene said as I opened the passenger door to let her out after I drove her home. 'Thank you for a lovely night.'

I leaned in to kiss her and once again, I felt like crying. She smelled of clean laundry and flowers, her lips were so soft and I was afraid to squeeze her in case I might hurt her, she was so delicate. The kiss went on for a long time and I was breathless by the time we pulled apart.

'Thank you, Irene,' I said, my voice cracking a bit. 'Can we go out again soon?'

We arranged to meet up again a couple of days later and this time I took her to one of my favourite places, a club with a massive dance floor. Irene was very impressed with the suit I wore that night, and even more impressed when I took to the floor and showed off my dance moves.

'Misspent youth,' I told her, giving her a wink after she asked me how I could dance like that, 'and a love of music. Anyone can dance if they let their body be taken over by the music, it's easy.'

'Easy for you,' Irene said. 'Me and Linda have to practice in the kitchen before we come out and if Linda's not there, I practice using a chair back!'

She was funny and so innocent. I never spoke to her about how I made my living, and she never asked. I'd have hated her to think of me as a violent man and over the next few weeks, I kept that side of me well away from her. Of course, my associates and friends would often want to speak to me about settling something or other, but they knew to be perfect gentlemen if I was out with Irene.

They would mind their manners and wouldn't swear in front of her, otherwise I'd have gone nuts. The only thing I could do on occasions like this would be to send Irene home, away from any bother, tucked safely into a taxi. Not once did she complain and not once did she ask why. She was the perfect girlfriend and I wanted to wrap her up in cotton wool. I couldn't get enough of her.

Within just a couple of months, I wanted my Mum and Dad to meet Irene. My older brother John was in the Navy now and away from home a lot, and my little brother was still in junior school. I just knew they'd all love my Irene as much as I did.

'That will be lovely, Mick,' my Mum said. 'I'll put some nice sandwiches on and a couple of cakes. Invite her round for afternoon tea.'

'I will, Mum,' I said, 'and you're going to really like her. She's gorgeous and she's such a lady, reminds me a lot of you to be honest.'

Mum and Dad both laughed, it tickled them to see me so worked up about a girl, but I know they loved seeing me happy. They probably thought that this one might be the one that turned my life around.

I think I thought that too.

CHAPTER FIVE

IRENE

I WAS nervous as hell when Mick took me home to meet his Mum and Dad. It was the first time I'd ever been invited to meet a boyfriend's parents and I didn't know what to expect.

'Behave, you little looney!' Mick said to me, after I'd told him how scared I was. 'They're just normal people, like me and you. They're going to love you, especially my little brother, Mark, he asks me loads of questions about you when I'm getting dressed to take you out.'

'Like what?' I asked, even more nervous now. 'Oh my god, Mick, what have you told them about me?'

Mick laughed and gave me a hug.

'Settle down, Princess, they know how much you mean to me and they love you already.'

In the end, I had nothing to be afraid of. His Mum and Dad were so welcoming, and such lovely people, I immediately felt at home. His little brother was so sweet too, always smiling and very polite, just like Mick. Before long I was sitting down with little Mark, helping to crayon with him in his colouring book. It was lovely and I felt that I belonged.

We spent lots of time with the family after that and I got to know Mick's Nan and Grandad too, who lived just a few doors away. They were such a close family and they always seemed so happy. I never heard an argument in that house. Sometimes, Mick and I would babysit for Mark and we'd spend the evening eating takeaway food and watching movies. I really loved those nights. Often I'd stay over and when I'd get up, everyone else had gone to work or school, but I'd feel so much at home that it didn't bother me in the slightest. I'd tidy round then wait for young Mark to come home at lunchtime and make him something to eat.

'Let's colour, Irene,' Mark would say, grinning at me. 'I'll do you a lovely picture while my soup warms up.'

He was such a lovely boy and, like Mick, I could never say no to him.

My own family, however, were starting to get worried about me.

'You're barely here, Irene,' Mum said one day as I was helping her wash the pots, 'and when you are, you're getting ready to go out. You're burning the candle at both ends, lovey, and that's not good for you, you must be shattered.'

'I'm fine, Mum,' I said with a sigh. 'You don't see me skiving off work, do you? I get my jobs done around the house and Mum, I love Mick. In fact, I'm in love with him. You want me to be happy don't you?'

'That's the trouble, Irene, me and your Dad only want what's best for you and, well, it's a worry for us when you stay out all night. It's not right. Our Rod and your Dad have been hearing rumours too, about Mick, about him getting into trouble with the police before. It's a worry, it really is.'

I was getting cross now, I hated it when I thought people were trying to put me off my Mick.

'And since when did we listen to rumours, Mum, hey? You've always laughed off local gossip, so what's different now? They can go to hell for all I care with their bloody rumours, and as for being out all night, you know where I am, at Mick's house, and Mr and Mrs Peterson are very strict about looking after me properly, you have nothing to worry about.'

Mum sighed and sat down at the kitchen table.

'I know you're a sensible girl, Irene, just please, look after yourself, and don't give the gossips anything to talk about.'

I wasn't lying when I said about the Petersons looking after me. Other than when they had a night out and we were left to babysit Mark, we rarely had any moments of privacy for a cuddle and a kiss, there was always somebody around, so I was really happy when my friend Linda moved into a shared house in Bromborough. She told me that me and Mick could go stay there as often as we liked. I couldn't wait to tell Mick the next time I saw him, I just knew he'd be as thrilled as I was.

However, something was wrong. For some reason, Mick stopped contacting me. It went on for days, and the days turned into weeks. I was so upset, wondering what I'd done wrong, and then I got angry to think he could just leave me like that.

At first I was traipsing the streets searching for him, but then I wouldn't leave the house and I refused to talk to Mum and Dad about it, I was devastated. Then, just as I was about to lose all hope, one of Mick's friends called to see me.

'I'm sorry to be the one to tell you, Irene,' he said. 'But the reason you haven't seen Mick for a while is that he's been locked up.'

'Locked up?' I asked, confused. 'What on earth do you mean? Locked up where?'

'He's done two months in Risley Remand Centre,' he said. 'For burglary and something about a car. He's due out any day now I'm not sure on all the details but, Irene, if I were you, I'd think twice about having him as your boyfriend.'

But I was over the moon! He hadn't just left me at all, he'd had no choice, of course he hadn't. I reprimanded myself for even thinking he'd just drop me like that. The reasons behind his absence were irrelevant to me, all I could think of was that my Mick was coming back to me, and we had Linda's flat to celebrate in.

I made such a fuss of Mick when he phoned to meet me and I couldn't wait to tell him all about the flat.

'I've stayed over a couple of times,' I told him. 'When I had the odd night with Linda, and guess what, Mick?'

'Tell me, you little looney,' Mick said, laughing at my excitement.

'There's a basement,' I said, 'and it's all painted black with loads of little lights and candles. Some of Linda's other friends rent that bit, but they have parties down there all the time, raves and the like.'

'Oh, raves and the like,' Mick said, still laughing. 'Well, we'll have to go see this flat then, hey?'

Mick was back, I was happy, and life was good again. I started to stay over at Linda's more and more often and Mick would spend time with me there before leaving to go home, but he'd always pick me up in the morning to take me to work, always the perfect gentleman. Eventually, I moved in properly and started paying towards the rent. It was then I told Mick that it was fine if he stayed overnight, seeing as I was now paying my way.

'Are you sure, baby?' He asked, cupping my chin with his hands. 'We can wait a bit longer if you like. I love you, Irene, but I don't want to push you into anything.'

'I'm sure, Mick,' I said. 'I really want you to stay.'

The first time we slept together, I was both nervous and embarrassed. I'd never seen a naked man before, and I was surprised to see he had a hairy chest, and he was so muscular. Despite my nerves, Mick really took care of me and my nerves soon calmed down. It was so special and I don't think I'd ever loved him more than I did that night, I felt complete.

Mick started to stay over more often after that and I loved it, it was like we were an old married couple. In fact, the only bugbear was that both me and Mick were very houseproud, but other residents in the building, not so much.

The couple across the hall would let every stray cat in the area shelter in there, it began to stink of cat pee, and they'd also leave the sink and table in the communal kitchen piled up with dirty dishes and takeaway cartons, it really got on my nerves.

'I'll help out more, baby,' Mick said one morning. I was getting upset as I couldn't find a cup for my tea. 'You're the first out to work every day and the last one home, it's not fair you have all this shit to come home to.'

'You do enough as it is,' I said, smiling up at him. 'Do you know, Mick, you remind me of Desperate Dan this morning, with all those whiskers.'

Mick laughed and rubbed his unshaven chin.

'What? I thought I'd grow a Mr Magoo beard for you,' he joked, and then kissed me. 'I haven't had time for a shave yet have I my little loon? Now you go get ready for work, leave this kitchen to me, girl.'

It was a relief really, because it had started to wear me down, having to clean a full kitchen the minute I got home from work before I could cook anything for us, but Mick kept his promise. From then on, I came home to a gleaming, spotless kitchen and to a boyfriend whose only purpose in life seemed to be to want to make me happy. I was such a lucky girl and I knew it. Even Linda, who by now was going steady with Mick's best mate John, pointed out how blessed I was.

'You should see his face, Irene, when you nip out to the shop or anything,' she giggled. 'It's like you've just told him you're off to Australia or something! I swear, he looks so sad and he wears the bloody carpet out pacing by the window till he spots you coming back, it's so funny.'

I laughed. 'That's because he loves me so much, he's my Desperate Dan, bless him.' We were having a quick tidy up of the living room and I was plumping some new cushions I'd bought from the market.

'I'm happy for you, Irene,' she said, 'and I'm happy with my John. I think it's fair to say we've both found our Mr Right.'

'We have,' I said, as I stood back to admire the newly adorned sofa, 'and you know, I'm as bad as him really. When he and John go off together for an evening and stay out all night, I get so worried and stressed out, I can't wait for him to get home.'

I never asked Mick where he and John went to late at night and Mick never said. I knew they were both busy men who worked hard, so it made sense to me that Mick might choose to work odd hours so that he could spend more time with me when I was home. He always made up for not being there too, he would leave little notes lying around for me to find after he'd gone. It always made me smile to find a little folded piece of paper under the pillow or in the sugar bowl, and even tucked into my sand-wiches that he'd sometimes make for me to take to work. It was always a love note saying, *I love you, my Princess*, or something equally lovely, and it made my day.

One day, though, I was unsettled because Mick and John hadn't gone off to work that morning. Mick had stroked my hair and kissed my head and told me I mustn't worry but they had to appear in court later for something silly that had happened a while ago.

I stared up at him, trying to gauge if I really ought to worry.

'Will it all be okay, Mick?' I asked, suddenly remember-ing the time I didn't see him for eight weeks. But rather than laugh and tell me I was his little looney, he looked sad and kissed my head again.

'Hopefully, baby,' he said. 'I'm really hoping so.'

I couldn't rest all day. I couldn't go to work, and instead

I went round to Mick's parent's house, only to find his Mum was just as worried as I was.

'He's just been a silly boy in the past, Irene,' his Mum said when I tried to ask how serious it was. 'But I tell you what, I'm going to make his favourite steak and onion pie for his tea, because that's how sure I am he will come back to us.'

Thankfully, Mick did come back to us that day and we all enjoyed the delicious pie together, chatting over tea about how Mick's older brother was due home on leave from the Navy in a few days, and how we could all make it special for him.

CHAPTER SIX

MICK

I DON'T think I'd ever felt such rage as when I was sat across the desk from my solicitor, listening to him say I was getting banged up.

'Nothing I can do about it, Michael,' he said, shuffling his fucking stupid briefcase around with his feet. 'They want to hold you on remand while they apply for further reports. I can't imagine it will be for long though, just a few weeks and then I'm positive we can get you off with a suspended sentence when it goes to court.'

I leaned towards the brief and looked him in the eye while he squirmed in his seat.

'It doesn't matter how fucking long, what matters is that they're locking me away from my fucking life knowing full well I'll get off with it in court. Why should they do that?'

'I'm just preparing you, Michael,' he said, standing up and walking towards the door. 'They've told me they're asking for you to be remanded. I can object, but I have to be honest, I don't stand a chance because there were too many witnesses to the crime.'

The useless bastard was right and the courts decided to remand me for eight weeks. Eight fucking weeks and I'd never even had the chance to explain anything to Irene. They sent me to Risley Remand Centre in Cheshire. Grisly fucking Risley. It was disgusting as far as prisons go, a filthy hole of a place, and it was home to some right doylems. But, home it was, at least for the near future, and as much as I wanted to smash the place up and everybody in it, the thought of my lovely Irene was enough to keep me from going mad. It tormented me every day that she'd be wondering where I'd gone, but I didn't want to contact anybody or see anyone, so I couldn't get word to her.

As the days went slowly by, I tried to adjust my brain into accepting that she might move on and forget about me, but it was no good, I just couldn't allow myself to picture that at all. I'd lay in bed in my cell and let all kinds of thoughts invade my head.

Why did she never ask what I was up to? How did I get so lucky to have such an angel fall in love with me? What if some bastard told her about my criminal activities and she decided I was no good? And the most tormenting question of all: *why was I never fucking happy with what I had, why did I always go out looking for more?*

I had no answers, other than I was born this way, always ready for action, attracted to danger and the unpredictable. It depressed me to think like this and I tell you, I cried like a fucking baby when word got to me that an old mate had visited Irene and told her where I was. But apparently, she had been over the moon, and couldn't wait for me to get out. That's all I needed to hear to get through it. Suddenly Risley wasn't so grisly anymore, because my Irene still wanted me. I was one lucky bastard.

I sailed through the rest of my time in there and it didn't even bother me that I was released on bail and still had the court hearing to attend. I'd been given a lifeline in Irene, and I intended to hold on to it.

'Listen, Irene,' I said as soon as we met up in person. 'I'm really sorry, baby, I just…'

'Stop that, Mick,' she said, smiling up at me with those eyes I could drown in. 'We've both been through a horrible time, but it's over now and we're together. Let's just put it behind us and be happy. Now, where are you taking me, my Desperate Dan?'

I stroked my chin automatically, then I scooped her up into a hug and spun her around. 'Well, the dancefloors of Ellesmere Port must have been missing us, Princess, let's go!'

That night we laughed almost the whole evening. It was as if we'd never spent a day apart and not once did Irene mention my time away. She was a first-class diamond and I was so grateful. She seemed tougher too in some way, as if she'd grown up some, but that just added to her charm.

Irene was certainly a chatterbox and I loved the sound of her voice, her tinkling laugh and her excitement about something that interested her. I was happy to just listen as she caught me up on the weeks I wasn't there. Linda's new flat, the big house, the couple opposite, the stray cats and the party basement. More accurately, the lads that lived in the party basement. That prickled me a little bit and I made a mental note to find out who they were and if they posed any threat to my Irene. But she made it clear that this flat was somewhere that we could really be alone at last.

It was a couple of weeks later that we first made love. I knew Irene was still a virgin, and I was honoured that she wanted me to be her first, but for the first time ever, I was nervous. She was so delicate, so precious, and I didn't want her to feel violated or pushed into anything. I actually thought she was going to bolt the first time we undressed to get into bed, she looked terrified. But in the end, there was no fear, no nerves, it was simply the most natural thing in the world, and the first time I understood the term 'making love'. This wasn't just me getting my leg over to serve a purpose, this was different. Once again, I had this mad need to start blubbing. Why did this woman make me want to cry?

Once I got the layout of the big, shared house, I began to see that my Irene was suffering. She worked all fucking day like a little Trojan, then had to come home and start cleaning. The dirty fuckers opposite Linda's flat would nick her food from the shared fridge, use every bastard pot and pan in the shared kitchen, fill the bins with their rubbish, then leave it all for poor Irene to sort out when she got home. Rather than cause a ruck, when I stayed overnight, I took to setting my alarm clock for an hour before Irene woke up so I could go clean the kitchen. I'd wash everything up, sweep and mop the floor and wipe round all the surfaces, just to make my Princess smile. I hated seeing the pained look on her face when she had to face all the shit first thing in the morning. I'd leave her 'I love you!' notes in the tea caddy or the sugar bowl too, just to make her happy.

I didn't mind doing all that for my Irene, but there were others living in that house too, and I wasn't about to let them mug me off. The filthy fuckers opposite had let all the feral cats in and the house was starting to reek of piss, so I decided enough was enough and I needed to have a word.

'Listen, you dirty bastard,' I said to the bloke opposite when I copped for him one morning. 'I'm only gonna tell you once.' I pointed towards the room we were discussing. 'That kitchen best remain spotless. Do you think I'm some kind of fucking mug?'

The man looked terrified as he shook his head. I wouldn't mind, I never laid a hand on him.

'Right, well if my Irene has to come home one more

time and start having to clear your shit up, then me and you will be having more than words, do you understand?'

I never told Irene I'd done that, and she thought the couple had suddenly decided to follow my example and start cleaning. She was thrilled about it, so I let her believe it. I had a word with the lads down in the basement, too, another thing Irene never knew. Their early hours of the morning raves only happened on the weekends after that. Anything to make my baby's life easier.

Life was really good, and even when I went to court for sentencing my stars must have been aligned or something 'cos I got off with probation. I'd left it right till the last minute before telling Irene about the court date because the truth was, I didn't want to worry her for a long period. It was bad enough her stressing out for just that one day.

After court, me and John vowed we would be more careful about our activities. The last thing I wanted was to get a tug by the coppers again and end up in jail, and by now we were heavily involved in debt collecting. We were paid really good money to pay visits to scumbags who owed bad men a lot of money and were late paying it back. We had a good routine going where we donned our best suits, knocked at the door of a house and then barged our way in. John would stand by in case there was anybody else around who might fancy their chances and I'd give the perpetrator a good hiding. It usually ended up with me collecting a payment or at the very least, if they had nothing on them, a threat to come back the next day. We never failed to collect and that meant we were on excellent commission. It was a good earner, and a no-lose crime to be honest, because these people were bad people, so there was never a chance they'd go to the police to report us.

AUTHOR OVERVIEW

MICK PETERSON

USING A retrospective understanding of Mick's situation and relationships, I have been able to make some professional observations.

A report on Mick at this time, might have read as follows:

Mick is in a complex relationship with Irene, a woman from a comfortable background not dissimilar to his own. The dynamic between them is marked by his obsessive love for her and his concealed criminal lifestyle. This report delves into Mick's mental and emotional state, assessing his behaviours and feelings.

ASSESSMENT PROCESS:

Initial Interviews: Communication with Mick was by letter and in person to discuss his relationship with Irene, his feelings about her, and his early criminal activities. It is evident that his affection for her is intense, bordering on obsession. He seemed anxious about her opinion of him, which is a common thread throughout our conversation.

Emotional Assessment: Mick expressed a belief that he must hide his criminal past to keep Irene's love. He described his feelings as a mix of euphoria when he's with her and despair when he thinks about the possibility of losing her. This emotional roller coaster is likely contributing to his mental strain.

Relationship Dynamics: We explored how Irene perceives him. Mick mentioned her oblivion to his criminal activities, which he feels is partly due to her privilege. This dynamic creates a sense of guilt and pressure for Mick, as he believes he has to maintain the illusion of being someone he's not.

FINDINGS:

Obsessive Love: Mick's feelings for Irene appear to cross the line into obsession, where his self-worth seems heavily dependent on her affection.

Avoidance of Truth: He avoids discussing his criminal past, fearing it would jeopardise their relationship. This avoidance may lead to increased internal conflict and anxiety.

Denial of Reality: There's a significant disconnect between Mick's criminal behaviour and his desire to be seen as a good partner by Irene. This state of denial can lead to harmful consequences if not addressed, as it masks an underlying fear of Irene discovering the violent side to his nature and ending the relationship.

We know, of course, that no such report was ever composed, nor did either Mick or Irene ever seek any form of counselling on their relationship.

People in those days tended not to. The attitude back then was still very much a 'what goes on behind closed doors, stays behind closed doors' attitude, even though the world was changing fast and women had much more freedom and far more rights than back in the 50s and early 60s.

When Irene met Mick, it suddenly seemed to her that he was everything she had been waiting for. An air of mystery that she never wanted to shatter a man who knew the ways of the world and who swept her off her feet. It was an instant attraction and it gave Irene everything she had been seeking. Validation that she was special and loved, the excitement of knowing that her suitor was revered, respected and feared, and the thrill of never knowing where he went, what he was doing and when she might see him again. Nobody could have convinced Irene that

Mick wasn't the man for her. Even when it became clear that Mick was obsessed with her, that only served to prove to Irene how much he loved her.

Mick admits that he always felt he was born ready for action. His family and upbringing were perfectly normal. He was also brought up quite privileged given the times and never remembers wanting for anything. But as a boy, he felt the same stirrings that Irene did; he wanted more than a normal life. He always had the feeling that the elusive 'big thing' he was always seeking was just around the corner and, as he grew up and got involved with crime, he started to think that perhaps this was his calling. He enjoyed the unpredictability and the possibility of getting caught doing something he shouldn't – and he enjoyed devising ways that would keep him one step ahead of the law, but still he had a gnawing feeling that something was missing.

When he met Irene, he was torn. He wanted her badly and he thought she might be exactly what he had been searching for. He had never met anyone like her, so beautiful and unspoiled and so innocent to anything bad in the world. He thought that having something so good in his life would surely outweigh any bad that was there. Without thinking any further than that, Mick made the leap and decided to see where it took him. His choice of career however already had him in a grip that he couldn't shake, but he told himself he could have it all.

Irene was naive and sweet, would never question him,

and accepted that the spoils of crime could provide them with a very happy life. That's exactly when life would have become problematic for Mick, because he would have to suppress a lot of who he really was in order to keep Irene happy… and yet that's exactly what he did.

CHAPTER SEVEN

IRENE

EVERYONE HAD always said that I had some strange ways, and I knew I did. It was little habits like touching ornaments or door handles a certain amount of times before I'd leave for work. I'd have routines such as turning certain light switches on before others, and only ever cleaning up in a certain order. I was always this way, but coming up to my first year in the flat, it got noticeably worse.

'What are you doing, Princess?'

I flinched and turned around to see Mick had woken up and was watching me tapping the little ornaments on my bedside table.

'Oh, you know what I'm like,' I said, 'but you've made me lose count now, Mick, shush! While I start again.'

'Little Looney,' Mick said, 'you know you're doing more and more stuff like this, don't you, baby? Is everything alright?'

I was getting annoyed now, because that was twice he'd made me lose count, and I couldn't start to get ready for work till I'd tapped each bloody ornament five times. I ignored Mick and started again, really quickly this time to get it over with.

'Might be worth nipping to see the doc, Irene,' he said after a few minutes to allow me to finish. 'I'm not saying there's anything wrong, baby, but it's worth having a word with him. I once had a mate that did things like you do and all it turned out to be was stress, but he got better after seeing the doctor.'

'I'm fine, Mick,' I said, 'but yes, if it makes you happy, I'll see the doc on my next day off, okay?'

Mick patted my bum and jumped out of bed, grinning.

'Good girl,' he said. 'Now I'm off to the kitchen to make you a cup of Rosie Lee, and I'm going to use a chipped cup.'

'Don't you bloody dare!' I yelled, laughing as he left the room.

Later that day I was lying on the bed, reading a magazine while I waited for Mick to finish work and I heard knocking at the door. Nobody else was home so I hurried to answer.

'Lucky heather, sweetheart?' An old Gypsy lady asked as she waved a sprig of the fragrant blossom in front of me.

I smiled at her and asked if she could wait a moment while I got my purse.

'Congratulations, sweetheart,' she said, smiling and then suddenly placed one of her bony hands onto my stomach. 'It's a little boy, it is. Oh! He's ever so lucky, I can see you standing over his crib.' She looked up at me. 'Well done,' she said. 'He's beautiful.'

Needless to say, without telling Mick, I rang work the next day to tell them I was sick and I went to the doctors. Of course, deep down I already knew that I was pregnant. My mood had been swinging a lot lately, my habits had worsened, and of course the Gypsies don't get it wrong, so it was no surprise to me when the doctor confirmed it.

I decided, as I walked home from the surgery, that of course I'd tell Mick and his family straight away, but I didn't want my own family to know just yet. My Mum and Dad still weren't keen on the idea of me being with Mick, probably due to the local gossips, so I wasn't going to add fuel to the fire by announcing I was pregnant.

'Oh my god, Irene!' Mick yelled as he picked me up and hugged me. 'Are you sure? I mean, course you're sure, what am I like, eh? But, oh baby! I'm going to be a dad!'

I laughed at Mick's enthusiasm, but somehow, I'd known he would be over the moon about it. I didn't know how I'd contain him for the next seven months though, because he could hardly wait, he was so excited. His parents were thrilled too and his Mum got me in the kitchen and confessed how relieved she was that he seemed to be settling down now. She said she had everything crossed that he'd stay out of trouble now for the sake of me and the baby. I told her she had nothing to worry about and that Mick didn't get into trouble these days. I didn't mention that I still worried now and again about what he was up to when he wasn't at Linda's flat though. He was still only spending half the week with me, and the other half with his parents.

As my pregnancy progressed and I guess I was overloaded with hormones, I started to get anxious when Mick wasn't there with me. He was so great when he was there and would bring me all kinds of things to put away in our 'bottom drawer', for when we eventually found our own place. He bought pots and pans, towels, kettle and toaster, everything you could think of, just to make me happy, but still I'd moan at him if he was late or decided to stay at his Mum and Dad's.

One evening, I was feeling particularly annoyed as Mick had promised to be home for tea and he was hours late. I was so mad that at 10 o'clock I locked the flat door so he couldn't walk in, then sat and waited for him to knock.

'Irene! The door's locked!' He shouted up through the letterbox.

I pushed open the big bedroom window and shouted back, 'You're not bloody getting in here, mister, not tonight!'

'Oh, come on, Princess,' he pleaded, smiling up at me. 'Let me in, I can explain why I'm late.'

'Don't Princess me,' I yelled, 'and I'm not bloody interested.'

'Well, I'm not going anywhere,' Mick said, 'so you might as well unlock this door now, I'm freezing.'

I walked away from the window, then before I could stop myself, I'd dragged a whole pile of things from our bottom drawer. Things we'd taken ages to buy, and I threw every single one of them out of the window, hitting Mick with the toaster on the side of his head. I scowled at him and then slammed the window shut. That'll teach him, I thought to myself, before throwing myself onto the bed and crying tears of self pity.

I felt a little bit sheepish when I woke up the next morning, and I wished I hadn't overreacted in that way. I knew I was hormonal and it was so annoying. One minute I was filled with love, the next I was raging. I didn't like it at all, and it was no surprise that I burst out crying before setting off to work. There had been a note pushed through the door from Mick, apologising and telling me how much he loved me. He'd even written a beautiful poem which ended in him asking me to marry him! It was so romantic and I couldn't wait to see him again to tell him I'd love to be his wife. It didn't matter that we'd done it back to front and I was pregnant first, all that mattered was that I was going to marry the man I loved with all my heart.

It was an exciting time for both of us, and Mick was just as into the arrangements as I was. Together we went to Chester Register Office to book our wedding for the beginning of January, then I went shopping and bought myself the most gorgeous white mini dress with batwing sleeves and a hood with white fur around it. Mick loved it and then surprised me by buying me a small white bible to match and to carry with me for the ceremony. He was so attentive and looked after me so well. Always cooking me meals and making me rest up after a hard day at work, it made me want to do more for him.

'Oh, baby, you shouldn't have gone to all this trouble,' he said to me one day when I had some time off. I'd made him his favourite sandwiches, taken the bus and turned up at the building site where he was working to surprise him.

'Don't be silly, it's no trouble,' I said, 'I love to see you, and you do so much for me, Mick, it's the least I can do.'

'That's why you're my little Princess,' he said, 'and don't forget it's Wednesday, my Mum is doing you some liver and cabbage again. She said it's really good for the baby.'

I laughed. His Mum, Eira, insisted I eat this at least once a week to up my iron intake, she was almost as obsessed with this pregnancy as Mick was. It made me feel a little guilty, though, that I still hadn't told my own Mum. Bless Mum, I really was ballooning by now and looked like I had a football underneath my clothes, but when we'd been out shopping together the day before, she simply commented that I was getting fatter since I'd left home. She genuinely didn't know and, for some reason, I didn't tell her. I also never mentioned the wedding and because Mick hadn't bought me an engagement ring – only a beautiful wedding ring to save for the big day – she had no clue about that either.

I was too scared to tell her if the truth be told. Not because either of them would do anything to me, but because my Dad was so strict and so set in his ways. I was his 'babbi' and I didn't want to upset or disappoint him. He didn't like Mick and I couldn't convince him otherwise.

As the weeks went by, and I was getting bigger, I realised I'd have to leave my beloved job at Littlewoods Pools. I was so sad to go and a lot of my workmates were sad I was leaving them. They all insisted on buying me presents to remember them by, but I told them all I needed were things for the baby.

'In blue,' I insisted, as I patted my swollen belly. 'Because I just know I'm having a boy. Don't ask me how, but I know.'

On the day I left, Mick came to pick me up and he was amazed at the huge pile of gifts I had to take home. Absolutely everything you could think of that one would need for a new baby. From tiny, blue sleepsuits and socks to bottles, dummies and outfits that would fit him for the first few months of his life. I was ever so grateful.

'They done you proud, Princess,' Mick said, grinning. 'Our boy is going to have everything and more, I promise you. Now come on, let's get you home. Long lie-ins for you from now on, my girl, you'll need all your strength soon enough.'

'You do look after me, Mick,' I said, smiling happily as I got into the car. 'I do love you.'

I was so happy and so looking forward to our wedding before the baby came. In fact, the only thing that was niggling at me was that I had the feeling something was going on with Mick and his mate, John. I wasn't sure what, but there were lots of whispered conversations late at night in the kitchen and they would stop talking if I walked in. I overheard talk of a train and guards, but I could never piece it together. I trusted Mick though, he'd promised me that everything was good, so I put it to the back of my mind. Even when a week or so later there was suddenly a lot of money to spend, I didn't question it. Everyone got flash new clothes and I was thrilled when Mick came home with yet another present for me.

'I bought you something, baby,' he said, passing me a large designer paper bag, 'and I know it's something you wanted because you were looking at them the other week and said they were too expensive. Well, nothing is too expensive for you, Princess.'

I opened the bag and squealed with delight, 'Oh, Mick! Thank you, thank you, thank you!' I cried, flinging my arms around him. 'It's the white boots!'

The beautiful, soft, white leather, zip-up boots I'd yearned for after seeing them in a shop window, I just couldn't believe he'd remembered, never mind bought them for me! I was over the moon.

'I'm going to wear them with my wedding outfit,' I announced. 'That's it complete now.'

'You'll look like a beautiful angel,' Mick said, 'just like you did on the night we met.'

Our wedding was a small affair as I didn't want anything flash, I just wanted to marry the man of my dreams. It was held at Chester Register Office on a cold, snowy day in January. I had invited my family, but I knew my Mum and Dad wouldn't come. My two sisters did though, and that made me feel happy. They had met up with Mick and his parents before coming to the service, and I felt so proud when Mick walked in, looking so smart in his beautiful, new, dark grey suit. We never bought Mick a ring, but mine was a gorgeous white gold band. I think we were both as nervous as each other because every time we attempted to say our vows, we glanced at each other and burst out laughing. It was so embarrassing and the poor registrar had to keep repeating himself until we were composed enough to do what we needed to.

After the ceremony we all went back to Mick's parent's house where we would now live together, at least until after the baby was born. We had a few drinks and some sandwiches and a lovely time, but after my sisters left, Mick pulled me to one side.

'Let's me and you sneak off for a few drinks,' he said. 'I

thought we'd go to The Bull, where we first met, you up for that, Princess?'

'Sounds good to me,' I said, smiling up at my new husband. 'I feel like the luckiest girl in the whole world.'

I can't even remember how many drinks I had that night, but we were definitely the stars of the show and we had such a laugh, I couldn't imagine how my life could get any better.

CHAPTER EIGHT

MICK

WHEN IRENE told me she was pregnant, I just couldn't believe it. I was going to be a dad. Me, a dad, it sounded mental and yet in that moment, it felt like a final piece of jigsaw was falling into place. I picked her up, tears in my eyes, and spun her around. I couldn't stop kissing her, her face, her head, her belly, I was like a fucking mad man really.

'I'm going to be the best dad ever,' I vowed, 'and our kid will want for nothing. I promise, Irene, I'm going to change my ways, get a decent job, and we'll get ourselves a lovely house. I'll save up and buy us the best of everything.'

'Steady on, Mick,' Irene said as she laughed along with my madness. 'You've always done alright by me, I'm not worried about anything, my love, and I'm only about two months gone, we've got plenty of time yet.'

As we lay in bed that night, I couldn't sleep. Irene was

fast on, snoring softly beside me, but my mind was like a fucking washing machine, whirring thoughts filling my head. For some strange reason I kept thinking about a time a few years earlier when I'd worked on a farm. I'd been working as a plasterer's labourer and we'd gone to do this big job for a farmer. My boss had gone to collect something we needed for the job, so I was at the door, having a tea break. Suddenly the farmer shouted at me from the cattle barn next door.

'Here lad,' he shouted, 'give us a hand out here, hurry up!'

I put my tea down and rushed to the barn where I saw him leaning over this cow that was laid on its side on the floor. It was letting out some right noises and was clearly in a lot of discomfort.

'What's up?' I shouted above the noise of the cow. 'What can I do?'

'Stuck calf,' the farmer replied, 'come round this end, lad.'

It was then I saw the calf's legs sticking out of the cow and the farmer had tied some rope to them. He was holding the other end of the rope to which he'd tied a long stick.

'Here,' he said, nodding at the stick, 'grab this with me, and when I say pull, you pull, when I say stop, you stop,' he looked up from the floor at me. 'You got that?'

I nodded and sat on the floor beside him, grabbing one

side of the stick. We both placed our feet on the poor cow's arse and started to pull.

'Pull! Stop! Pull! Stop!' The farmer was shouting as we did what needed doing. I couldn't believe what we were actually doing as I saw the calf coming further out of the cow. The poor cow was making one hell of a noise, all the other cows seemed to be watching us. Then suddenly, after one final pull, it came out, alive and shaking itself, I was in total shock and awe. The farmer grinned and slapped me on the back.

'Well done, lad, thanks for that.'

It was a moment that I'd remember forever, I'd actually helped to bring life into the world. It was such an amazing experience, and here I was, thinking about that as I watched my Irene sleeping beside me with another little miracle inside of her. I was responsible for bringing both a calf and a baby into this crazy, fucked up world, and I was exhilarated.

I was happy when Irene finished working when she started to get bigger, as it meant I could look after her properly. I don't know what it was, but I got really scared when she wasn't beside me, like it sent me into a panic thinking she didn't want to be with me. Even if she just hopped on the bus to go shopping, I'd wave her off but then my heart would be pounding in terror thinking I might never see her again or something. It was mad, but I couldn't help it. It was much better knowing she would be home every day now, and I couldn't do enough for her.

'You're so good to me, Mick,' she said one morning as I helped dry her after the bath, with a big, white, fluffy towel. 'But you know I am capable of drying myself.'

The night she locked me out of the flat was horrendous. I was begging her to let me in, but I knew I'd fucked up. Instead of going straight home after work, I'd gone to meet John at the pub to discuss a deal we were setting up for these gangsters, and time had just run away from us. She was like a raving lunatic at our window, chucking stuff down at me and the fucking new toaster clumped me on the side of my head. I decided best to fuck off to my Mum's and let her calm down a bit. My Mum gave me a telling off too, saying I was lucky to have Irene and if I wasn't careful she'd be off with someone more reliable. Fuck that. I wrote a proposal poem and in the early hours of the morning I went back to the flat and shoved it under the door for Irene to find when she woke.

I was surprised when Irene opted for a small affair for our wedding, but to be honest I'd have married her in a fucking phone box. I wasn't bothered that it was just the register office. When I walked in to see her standing there, waiting for me, I was so choked up. I'd never in my life felt so much love flood through my body than at that moment. She was a vision in white, a perfect angel, I felt like the luckiest bastard in the universe. We had a bit of a party at my Mum and Dad's house afterwards, then me and Irene went to celebrate at The Bull, where we'd first met. A kind of win-win for me because I had a bit of dosh to collect from a job me and John had done a few weeks prior.

That was becoming more difficult now that Irene wasn't working, doing my not-so-legitimate work as well as my regular day job on a building site. I was sure that Irene suspected I was up to no good, but she never asked and never commented. Seriously, I wanted to go fully legit, but we needed money for this new baby and a place of our own. I told myself that once we had all that sorted, I'd go completely straight.

It did become easier after the wedding though, when we moved into my parent's house, because Irene was happy for Mum to look after her when I wasn't there. She didn't stress about any of my late nights or weekends working because she always knew I'd be coming home to her. It was mainly smash and grabs we did, a fast way to nick a few stereos or TVs and then sell them on, and I really was fast, having honed my skills as a kid in my little gang. Then, of course, there were the lorries. We'd get word when a big store was due a good delivery, wait for our moment, then take the lorry and dump it, but not before we'd emptied its contents into our warehouse. But the fastest money was always debt collecting, and it also enabled me to let off steam, of course.

'You're a married man now, mate,' John said to me

one night after we'd beat up a particularly nasty fucker down by the docks, 'won't she wonder how your hands got bashed up?'

I glanced down at my torn knuckles and mused at how bad that fucker's face must be feeling, then I shrugged.

'She never does,' I said. 'I mean, she must notice, but she never says anything, and just runs me a bath and lays me some clean clothes out. She's a fucking diamond is my Irene.'

John laughed, 'It'll all change once you get your own gaff, mate,' he said. 'She's got your Mum to chat with now, but you watch, you're going to have to reign it in a bit when you move out of there.'

John was right, but move out we must. It was a squeeze at my Mum and Dad's house when my older brother came home on leave, and it'd be even more cramped when the baby came. I'd promised Mum that as soon as Irene gave birth, I'd have us something sorted. We'd already put our names down with the council for a house in Ellesmere Port. Irene loved it there and it was close to my Nan and Grandad's, so she'd still have the support if she needed it, but it wouldn't be like when she lived at the flat and I could tell her I was staying at Mum's for a couple of nights. Once we'd gone, we'd gone, and I'd have nowhere to use as an alibi home.

When baby Michael was born, I was completely and utterly in love with him. He was just perfect. My Mum was all over him and said he looked just like I did when I was a baby. Poor little fucker, I thought. But another great thing that happened after he was born was that Irene's Mum and Dad came around to the fact that we were together. They fell instantly in love with baby Mike and promised to be there for my Irene whenever she needed them. Both sets of parents offered to babysit any time we wanted, and when we finally got offered our own council house, I think they were all a bit disappointed that we'd be leaving and looking after ourselves from now on.

CHAPTER NINE

IRENE

I WAS so happy when we got the keys to our own, new house. I felt so grown up and I could tell that Mick was just as excited.

'Come on, baby,' he whispered to me one morning as baby Mike was sleeping in his crib by the side of the bed. 'Mum's going to watch our Mike, and me and you are off to Ellesmere Port, shopping.'

'Oh!' I said, grinning as I leapt out of bed. 'Things for the house?'

'Anything you like for the house,' Mick said, throwing a lime green mini dress at me to put on.

'We need furniture and everything else and John's told me about this shop in town where you can get anything on HP, so come on, hurry up before it gets busy.'

I'd heard of HP before, it meant hire purchase, and it was a way of buying something and paying for it over time, like a year or two years. My friend, Joanne from work, had once furnished her full house doing this, so I was thrilled.

'Yes!' I said, pulling the dress on and hopping around in the bedroom as I tried to slip into my new sandals. 'I've been writing lists of what we need, but Mick, I want all modern stuff, baby, all in white too. Oh! We'll have the best home in Ellesmere Port!'

I was in my element as I swanned around the big store and chose the most beautiful things for our new home. All ultra-modern too: a sleek, round, white coffee table, a huge, matching white wall unit with lots of shelves, drawers, wardrobes, dressing table, and the most amazing television I'd ever seen. It was also white, of course, with a round, pedestal stand, and the frame of the TV was round too. Mick laughed as I practically skipped around the place picking up coloured glass vases and other ornaments.

'Where are they all going to go?' He asked, shaking his head at my hoard.

'In the wall unit,' I said, 'a different colour vase in each little shelf, it will look fab!'

'Leave them with the assistant then,' Mick said, 'and she can wrap them for us. It's time to go up to the next floor, we still need carpets and wallpaper yet.'

'Oh, Mick,' I laughed, 'I think you'll have to do a bank robbery to pay for all this!'

Mick gave me a very odd look but then laughed too. 'Bank robbery? HP? Nothing too much trouble for my Princess,' he winked at the bemused shop assistant and then we headed up the escalator to the next floor.

White, of course, was the in thing that year, but so was vibrant colour, and I wanted a mix of both. I chose a gorgeous purple carpet and matching purple wallpaper for our living room, then a giant, black floor vase and some huge, colourful paper flowers. I really thought I was the bee's knees as I walked out of that shop with my repayment book tucked safely in my handbag, I was so happy and couldn't wait to get stuck in, decorating and arranging everything. Mick had already bought all the things we needed for little Mike's room, and I'd replaced all our bottom drawer things, so we were all set to go. We moved in the following week after a big van had turned up to deliver all our new stuff.

Our house was perfect, with small gardens at the front and side, and a huge back garden – all grass – that led directly to a big railway line. I got used to trains rumbling by and soon caught the gardening bug. I bought flowers to plant, seeds, and some little bushes. I couldn't wait for baby Mike to get older so he could play out in the garden and I could buy a sand pit and some swings for him.

I was very artistic and liked to keep myself busy, so I was forever buying little tins of colourful paint so that I could paint different types of flowers on the kitchen tiles and walls to brighten it all up. Mick had painted the walls a gorgeous orange colour already, so my flowers set it off lovely. One day, after I'd been particularly busy, I decided to have a nap while the baby was sleeping, but I was woken up to the sound of Mick shouting his head off from upstairs.

'What the fucking hell?' He shouted, 'Irene! What have you done?'

I was puzzled at first, having been woken up like that, and I ran to the bottom of the stairs, 'Mick?' I shouted, 'you alright, baby?'

Then I saw him and remembered instantly what I'd done. I burst out laughing and couldn't stop. The tears were streaming down my cheeks from laughing so much.

'Oh, Mick,' I said, when I could actually speak. It was funnier because he was standing naked, at the top of the stairs, covered in turquoise paint. 'You look so funny, love,' I laughed, holding my sides. 'I was asleep when you came in, but I painted the bathtub. I thought it would look nicer in a blue shade.'

'Nicer?' Mick spluttered, 'Princess, I'm coated in the stuff, I'll never get it off!'

It was hilarious. Apparently, the paint I'd used wasn't the right base for painting a bath and would always come off with the water. Mick hadn't even noticed the change in colour and just lay in it while he ran the taps. He saw the funny side, though, and we both laughed our heads off as I helped him scrub the paint from his body and the bathtub.

'It actually suits you, Mick,' I said as I scrubbed his back, 'with your tanned body and dark hair, at least we know now that turquoise is your colour.'

'Oh well, at least we know that then, eh?' Mick said, laughing again. 'Irene, next time you get the urge to paint, baby, run it by me first, okay?'

Another day I decided to decorate Mike's bedroom. I bought some rolls of wallpaper covered in little zebras and elephants. I'd never wallpapered before and was surprised, once I got started, how easy it was. You simply pasted the paper and then hung it on the wall. I'd seen Mick do it at his Mum and Dad's house, so I also knew to use a clean sponge to rub each strip down, in order to remove any air bubbles. I was really proud of myself when I finished, and couldn't wait for Mick to get home to see my handiwork.

'Follow me upstairs,' I said to Mick as soon as he got in from work, 'and close your eyes till I say open.'

'Sounds good to me,' Mick said, slapping my bottom and winking, 'get up those apples and pears!'

'Not that, you dirty sod,' I laughed, 'come see what I've done today.'

I led him along the landing by his hand, and into the baby's room. 'Open your eyes now,' I said. 'Tah dah!'

I watched Mick's expression as he stared at each of the

four walls in turn, and was surprised by his silence.

'Didn't I do well?' I urged, 'and I've never done it before.'

'Irene, baby,' he finally said, 'you do know that you're meant to pattern match each strip of paper, don't you?'

I stared at the walls too now, and suddenly realised why it had looked so abstract to me before. Half zebras and half elephants were now really obvious to me and I couldn't unsee them.

'Oh, yeah,' I said, feeling daft, 'does it look really bad do you think?'

Mick laughed and hugged me.

'No, baby, it doesn't, but promise me you'll leave the decorating to me from now on. You just add your little touches where you like, but I'll do the papering. Deal?'

Our life was far from perfect, but I loved it. The only blight, really, was that I started to resent Mick going out to the pub almost every day after work. Sometimes he didn't come home at all and that would send me raging. We had some furious rows, and I would shout at him from the top of my lungs. He'd try to shame me into shutting up by pointing out that the neighbours would hear and think I was some kind of fish wife, but that didn't bother me at all.

The couple to the right of us also had a small baby, but I soon learned that not every mother seemed to like being a mother. The woman used to go out almost every night, a bit like Mick, and then come home blind drunk, also like Mick at times. She would then have the most violent rows with her husband, who would try his best to keep the peace for the sake of their baby, but she would swear and throw things around, yelling at him that he was useless and a good for nothing. I felt so sorry for that husband of hers, having to put up with that, he seemed like a lovely man and a really good dad. He would always be the one pushing the pram to the shops or carrying their daughter to the park, while his wife would be recovering in bed all day. Perhaps he thought the same about me and Mick, because he must have heard our rows too.

Outweighing the bad moments, there always seemed to be lots of tender, sweet moments that kept me so happy to be married to Mick. We didn't own a lawnmower, so I would often wake up to hear Mick in the back garden, cutting all the grass with a big scythe. He had planted all the privet cuttings my Mum had given us, and he was careful to tend to them every day. He would love to come upstairs and stand with his arm around my waist, looking out of the bedroom window at our lovely garden. He was so proud of it, and so was I. However, I was left dumbfounded on morning, when I heard a noise from the garden and assumed it was Mick, so I looked out to see three sheep in there! They were eating all the grass and running around, I couldn't believe my eyes.

'I've no idea,' Mick said later when I asked about them, 'they must have gotten in through the bottom, near the railway lines, but at least they've done a job for me, I don't have to get the scythe out this week.'

I have to admit, I had some suspicions about those sheep and where they came from, but I never said anything. It was proof that Mick wanted to do things that made me happy. He would still leave little 'I love you!' notes in the sugar caddy and under my pillow too, so even when I got angry with him, it was never long before I forgave him. By now, Mike was toddling about all over the place and could go to the local nursery. Mick was working for a firm called Ellis and Perry, in Ellesmere Port, as an industrial painter. He had to scale some huge petrol storage tanks on industrial estates – it's a good job he was fit and agile.

To alleviate the boredom, I decided to go back to work too and got a job as a typist working for a firm who made and exported wooden pallets to South Africa. I never really settled there though, as I felt like I was being singled out by the female boss. She clearly favoured the other typist who had worked there for years, and it felt as if I was constantly being picked on. Every little mistake and I'd be shouted at, while the other girl would get a 'don't worry, sweetie, I'll help you sort it out'. I hated the woman.

CHAPTER TEN

MICK

I WAS making good money and our little boy was growing up fast. The only times me and Irene argued were when I never went straight home after work. She hated me drinking down the pub and would regularly put Mike in his pushchair and go out searching for me, so I often had to go further afield to avoid detection. I swear, the cops had fuck all on Irene when she was on a mission. I needed far more alibis for my Irene than I ever did for the filth. I loved the bones of her though, and hated it when she got upset and raged at me. I always tried to make it up to her, but she wasn't one of those women who would have been happy with a bunch of flowers and a box of chocolates, or even a new outfit and bits of gold. My Irene was at her happiest when I did something thoughtful for her.

One year she'd told me how at Christmas every year, her Mum would make her a stocking and fill it with fruit, sweets and small gifts. I could see in her eyes and expression how much that had meant to her, so I never forgot it and the next Christmas I made her a special stocking, just like her Mum had done. I put an apple and an orange in at the bottom, some silver chocolate coins, and then topped it with a gorgeous, purple silk nightie and negligee. Her little face lit up, she was so grateful and happy and, you know, even if I hadn't received anything that year, it was the best present I could ever have had.

Around the same time, Irene decided she wanted to go back to work, and although I didn't really want her to, I knew it was important to her. She'd always worked, long before she met me, so I had no right to argue about it now, but I did get very jealous if I saw her wearing her best clothes and make-up for the office.

'You look beautiful without all that shit on your face,' I said one morning as I watched her getting ready, 'and don't you think that dress looks a bit tarty for just going to work?'

Fuck me, she threw a hairbrush straight at me, and all hell broke loose.

'Don't you dare, Micky Peterson!' She yelled, 'don't you bloody dare! I'm sick to death of you telling me what to wear and how to look. I just like to look smart for work, is that a crime now?'

'Alright, calm down,' I said, rubbing the side of my head, 'you know how I get when you go off without me. You know that other men will look at you, Irene, they all do.'

'Well, I don't bloody look at them, do I? That's the point, Mick, I don't care who looks, because that doesn't harm anyone, does it? I belong to you and that's that.'

It would fucking harm them if I caught them looking, I thought, but didn't say.

I had no argument really because, truth be told, I'd bought her most of her clothes and fancy make-up in the first place, so it was stupid to now say she couldn't wear them. I decided to keep quiet, but I was really happy when she walked out of that job, I can tell you. It was a sad occasion, my Grandad's funeral, actually, and they told her she couldn't have time off. My Irene was a straight talker, and she took the day anyway leaving a letter for the boss saying what she thought of her. That was the end of that job. Happy me.

I'm a fool to myself though, always have been, and when things were good at home, I'd be happy enough to get busy with my extracurricular activities with John, or some of the other rogues I dealt with. My thinking was that life was too good for it to all come crashing down. The dangerous flip side was that when things weren't so good at home, I'd also want to go out and do stuff I shouldn't, but at these times, my head wasn't on straight enough to weigh up all the risks and take the necessary precautions. It was after a particularly bad argument with Irene that I did something that would change the course of my life forever.

'You are not going to the pub tonight, Mick, I mean it.'

Irene said as she watched me putting a new suit on. 'I'm sick of being left at home with just the baby for company, sick of it!'

I'd had a shit day at work and a big job we had planned for the weekend had fallen through, so I wasn't in the best of moods. I picked up the plate of pie and mash that Irene had made for my tea, which I'd left uneaten, and I threw it against the wall.

'Since when do you give me orders?' I yelled. 'I'm off to the pub to do some fucking business and that's that. It's a mother's job to look after her kid, what's wrong with you?'

I immediately felt bad when I saw Irene flinch. I couldn't believe I'd made her feel afraid, but that only served to make me feel even more angry at myself. I was about to apologise when Irene ran from the room and then came back with a handful of photographs.

'See these, you bloody pig,' she shouted. 'This is what they're worth to me.'

She then started to rip every single one of them to pieces. They were our wedding photos, I just couldn't believe it, and I saw red. I grabbed the bits of torn photos and threw them all in the kitchen sink, then I took a box of matches and set fire to them.

'Let me help,' I said, unable to think straight now, 'and tonight, I'll be staying out all night, by the way. I'll stay at my Mum's.'

I stormed out of the house, absolutely raging and walked

around the block to calm down before heading to the pub to meet with a couple of mates.

A couple of pints later, myself and three friends were holding up a shop. It was my sawn-off shotgun that I was holding, and it was me doing all the intimidating. We got what we wanted and fled the scene. For me this was therapy, a way of getting rid of the anger and shame I had for treating Irene the way I had, but somehow, I knew this time was different. Everyone on the scene knew it was me, and I knew the three accomplices wouldn't keep their traps shut if push came to shove. I had no choice, I'd have to go on the run to see if the heat would die down or word got to me that I was in the clear.

I went to my parent's house and stayed for the night as I knew I'd have a bit of time, but then I fucked off, staying here, there and everywhere trying to stay one step ahead. I soon got word that the others had been caught and that the coppers were after me, so a fortnight later, I went back to Mum and Dad's, knowing I'd be arrested within the day. After a few hours in Ellesmere Port Police Station, they sent me straight to jail on remand to wait for a High Court hearing.

CHAPTER ELEVEN

IRENE

AFTER I walked out of my job at the pallet place, I had a lot of extra time on my hands. Mike was already two and had been spending lots of time with his grandparents and Daddy while I worked and did the odd few sessions at nursery. But now I could have him home with me, which was lovely. I could pop him in his pram and take him to the park rather than Mick do it all the time. It had been lovely, of course, knowing that my husband and son were developing such a close bond, and little Mike used to squeal with laughter as his Dad swung him up onto his shoulders. They clearly loved their time together. But now, never one able to simply relax, I could do all that, as well as spend time keeping my beautiful home spick and span.

It also meant, however, that I started to see things I'd never noticed before. Things about Mick's life that, if I thought about it, would make me worry, so I tried to push it to the back of my mind for my own sanity. One day I heard knocking at the door while I was cleaning the kitchen. I glanced out of the window and could see Mick and Mike playing in the back garden with a football, so I dried my hands and went to the front door.

'Mrs Peterson?' The taller of the two policemen standing outside said.

'Yes,' I said, confused and worried that a family member must be hurt.

'We need to speak to your husband, Michael Peterson, if he's home. Don't worry, it's just a few questions.'

I was immediately worried, of course, and I asked them to come in and wait in the living room while I went out for Mick.

'Mick, there's policemen in our living room, love, what's going on?' I said as I scooped Mike up and wedged him onto my hip.

'You let them in?' Mick asked, incredulously. 'Baby, why did you let them in?'

'Because they're policemen, Mick, that's why,' I said, almost in tears. 'What's going on?'

Mick kissed my cheek.

'Don't worry, Princess, everything is alright, this must be a misunderstanding that's all, you take Mike upstairs and I'll sort it out. Go on.'

I waited until Mick had gone inside and then I followed. I knew he'd be angry if I went into the room with him, so

I took Mike into the kitchen and gave him a biscuit while I listened by the door.

'Leaving the scene of an accident,' one officer was saying, 'it's a criminal offence, Mick, you know that.'

'I done fuck all,' Mick said. 'Definitely wasn't me, mate.'

'The collision was between a Cortina and a car we know belongs to you, Mick, and we have a witness who gave your description. Can you show us your car?'

'I'm telling you, it wasn't fucking me,' Mick replied. 'I don't care what your fucking blind witness has said and as for the car, I don't even have a fucking car anymore. Got shot of it weeks ago!'

Well, that was partly true. The car had gone, but it had only been a couple of days ago, and Mick had told me he'd started leaving it at work. I decided to leave it at that though, I didn't want to make matters worse by questioning him after the police left, because after showing them out he was in a good mood and told me, 'See, baby, I told you it was all a misunderstanding, it's someone else they're looking for, not me.'

Another thing I noticed since being home all day was that Mick's drinking seemed to be escalating, or perhaps it had always been the same, but I hadn't noticed with being out at work all day. One day I was in a really good mood. Mick had been on his hands and knees, scrubbing the kitchen floor for me before going out to work, and I'd found a lovely note from him in Mike's biscuit tin. I decided I'd make a lovely roast for our tea, one of Mick's favourite meals, apart from steak pie. I set the dining table out really nicely and added a little vase of flowers I'd picked from the garden, and waited.

I fed Mike his tea at around 4.00pm as usual and let him watch some cartoons while I prepared ours, and I had it all plated up and served to the table for 5.00pm, but Mick didn't show up. I waited another 15 minutes before eating my own tea, afraid it would be too cold if I didn't, but I could barely swallow it, I was so angry. Little Mike saw me pacing and looking out of the window and he climbed onto a chair to look out with me.

'Daddy?' He asked, as we waited.

'Not tonight, darling,' I told him as I picked him up and carried him upstairs. 'Mike, have a nice bath and play with your duckies and then it's bedtime.'

It was around 5.00am when I was woken to the sound of Mick banging at the door, so I went down to let him in. He had a key of course, but he was so drunk that he couldn't manage it. When I opened the door it was to find Mick swaying from side to side, barely able to stand up, and a broken milk bottle on the step. I was so mad, but decided to leave it until he'd sobered up, so I locked the door, walked straight by him and went back to bed. It seemed like I'd only just drifted back to sleep again when I was woken with a jolt to hear a loud bang and Mick shouting and swearing from downstairs. I couldn't believe it when I went back down and saw the chaos he'd caused. His lovely dinner had been thrown at the wall, the coffee table was upturned and all the cushions from the sofa had been thrown around. He was just about to throw a glass vase at the television when I walked in.

'Mick!' I shouted, stopping him in his tracks. 'Give that to me, love, come on.'

He bloody smiled at me and put his arms out for a hug! 'Irene, my Princess,' he said, 'there you are.'

Deep breath, I told myself as I put my arm around his waist and helped him upstairs to bed. The next morning, I went down to make a cup of tea and I just sat on the sofa and waited for Mick to get up. I didn't move a thing because I wanted him to see what he'd done.

'My god, Irene!' He said when he eventually surfaced and looked around at the mess. 'Why, baby? What on earth possessed you?'

The cheeky bugger thought I'd done it in a fit of rage. I told him exactly what had happened, but he wouldn't have any of it, and swore blind he'd never do such a thing and, no matter how much I told him otherwise, he simply wouldn't believe it. He was in a state of shock, I think, as he helped me put the house back in order. He did say that he'd never drink that much again.

A couple of weeks later, on Friday evening, Mike and I were sitting watching TV, waiting patiently for Mick to come home with our tea. Fridays were paydays for Mick and every week, for a treat, he'd call at the Chinese takeaway and bring a feast home for us all so that I didn't have to cook. It was always just after 5.00pm when he walked through the door, but that time came and went, so did 6.00pm, and there was still no sign of Mick. I was getting really stressed, and both me and little Mike were starving. Where the hell was he? It was around 7.30pm when the door went and I leapt up, thinking it was Mick and that he'd lost his key or something, but no, it was his Dad, Joe, carrying a large takeaway bag.

'Your supper, love,' Joe said, handing the bag over to me. 'Our Mick asked me to get it for you, he's had to go into town, something important he said.'

I was furious, but I tried to keep everything normal for the sake of our Michael.

'Daddy's very busy at work, darling.' I told him when he cried because Mick wasn't there for our takeaway night. 'You'll see him tomorrow.'

He didn't, however. Nor the next day, nor the next. I was going out of my mind with worry, but I certainly didn't want to tell Mum and Dad, or Mick's parents. I felt stupid and kept it from everyone.

For the next few days, I'd put little Mike in his pram and we took more walks than we'd ever taken. Up and down all the streets looking for Mick's latest car. I'd look through the pub windows, hop on the bus to check out the pubs in town I knew he frequented, but he had simply disappeared, nowhere to be found. I was heartbroken and so afraid that something bad had happened.

'Where's Daddy, Mummy?' Mike would ask, daily.

'He's really busy, darling,' I'd reply, trying to smile though inside I was so scared. 'You know what a busy job he has, maybe we'll see him tomorrow, now be a good boy and I'll tell Daddy what a little soldier you've been.'

It was two weeks after he'd gone that I woke to hear the banging on the door at 2.30am. The relief that flooded through me replaced any anger or fear I'd been feeling. He's home at last, I thought as I grabbed my purple negligee and pulled it around me to let him in. But even after I'd switched the hallway light on, the banging continued. That was a bit strange, so I called out.

'Who is it? Who's there?'

'Mick,' came the reply.

Smiling, I unlocked the door only to have it pushed at me and the hallway was stormed by five policemen.

'What the hell is going on?' I yelled, terrified for little Mike, as four of the officers ran straight past me and up the stairs, shouting Mick's name.

The one officer who remained with me looked a bit shamefaced as I desperately tried to clutch my negligee around me.

'I'm sorry for this, Irene, is it? But we're looking for Mick.'

'He's not here,' I cried. 'I haven't seen him for a fortnight. What's he supposed to have done?'

'Can't really say,' the officer said, 'and I really am sorry, Irene, I happen to like Mick myself, we were at school together you know.'

I led him through to the living room, but was stressed about the others, still upstairs.

'Don't worry,' he said, 'they know there's a kid up there, they'll be quiet, but they have to search every room you see.' He then looked all around my living room and whistled, 'I tell you what, love, he's certainly given you a lovely home, that's good.'

The other officers came back down then, shaking their heads to show they hadn't found what they'd been looking for and they all left. I ran upstairs to find little Mike sitting up in his bed, crying.

'I'm scared, Mummy,' he said, rubbing his eyes. 'Was them bad men?'

'No, baby,' I said, 'just some men who used to live here and they'd left something behind, that's all, they came back to find it.'

If I'd have found Mick myself right then, I'd have bloody strangled him.

He was still missing the next day, so to console Mike, I took him to his favourite toy shop and bought him a little red lorry to play with. It was easy to distract the baby, not so much myself. The police hadn't just checked every room, they had pulled out every drawer and emptied its contents, the same with every cupboard. God knows what they were searching for, but it wasn't as if Mick might be hiding in a bloody drawer, was it? I didn't have the heart to even think about clearing it all up, my beautiful house felt soiled somehow, violated. I decided I needed to swallow my pride and get in touch with my Mum and Dad for help, so before I could change my mind, I grabbed a couple of coins from the bottom of my handbag and wheeled the pram straight to the phone box at the end of the road.

'Can me and Michael stay with you for a few days?' I asked Mum, 'I don't want to go into it, but Mick's gone on the run from what I can gather, I just don't want to be at home, Mum, the police have ransacked it.'

I waited for the telling off to come, the disappointed tone, but there was just silence for at least a minute. Then finally Mum said I should pack a few bits and they'd be with me soon.

My parents collected me an hour later, and I stayed with them until I felt strong enough to go back home and face the mess. Mum must have told Dad not to question me because they didn't mention either the state of my house or what had happened to cause it, for which I was grateful. I just didn't have the strength to pour my heart out to anyone. I couldn't stay forever though and, for all I knew, Mick could be home and out looking for me so, after three days, I decided that we had to go back.

I played out various scenarios in my head, one of which was that Mick was searching the streets for me and Michael, night after night, just as I had done for him. It was driving me mad.

But of course, Mick wasn't back, and by the state the house was still in, I knew he hadn't been in it. I took Mike round to Eira and Joe's house and asked if they'd watch their grandson for a couple of hours while I cleaned up. I didn't elaborate because I knew they were worried themselves and I didn't want to add to that. They were glad of the distraction I think as they made such a fuss of little Michael, picking him up and kissing him.

Tears sprang to my eyes as I turned and walked away, why did Mick have to be so unpredictable? We had such a happy life and a happy little boy, why couldn't that be enough for him?

I vowed that when Mick came home, he'd have to answer these questions, because as far as I was concerned, things had to change now. We couldn't keep putting our little lad through this.

I was almost done with my deep clean when I glanced out of the window to see Mick's Dad, Joe, walking down the path. He didn't have Michael with him so I assumed he must have come to invite me over for tea. I was happy about that as I was starving and needed a break.

'Hi, Joe, come in.' I said, smiling now that I was no longer ashamed of my messy house. 'Has little Mike been a good boy?' Only then did I notice the grave expression on my father-in-law's face.

'I'm so sorry, Irene,' he said, as he followed me inside. 'Sit down, love, there's something…'

'Joe, what is it?' I asked, my heart leaping around in my chest. 'Please, just tell me.'

'It's our Micky,' he said, 'he's been locked up, love, and you need to go see him. It's serious this time, Irene. He won't be coming home.'

CHAPTER TWELVE

MICK

IT BROKE my fucking heart when Irene came down to the cop station where I was being held before my transfer to jail. Thankfully it was in Ellesmere Port, so she didn't have far to travel, and I tried to prepare myself for seeing her. Don't break Micky, not in front of Irene, I told myself. I knew full well she would be at breaking point herself and I felt so guilty about that, because I'd caused every bit of it, but the moment the copper on guard led her in, any bravado I'd been clinging onto fucked off out the grill covered window.

'I'm so sorry, Irene, I'm so, so sorry, baby,' I said, as I looked into her sad eyes.

'Oh, Mick,' was all she said before she sat down and cried. 'What's going to happen to you? What's going to happen to us?'

I reached out to hold her hands.

'I love you so much, Princess,' I said, 'and Michael, I love you both more than anything. You know that, right?'

She looked up at me then, terrified and upset.

'Stop it, Mick, just stop it,' she cried, 'it sounds like you're saying goodbye to me.'

I've heard people talk about having a lump in their throat, and I always thought it was just a saying. But at that moment, I knew exactly what it meant. Fighting the urge to cry with every ounce of strength I had in me, I found it actually hurt my neck to force any words out.

'Baby, I could never say goodbye to you, ever, I hope you know that.' I said as I gripped her hands. 'And my solicitor reckons I have a good chance at the High Court, but for now, Irene, I have to go to jail on remand for a few weeks, just while it all gets sorted. Can you please look after yourself and our Michael for me while I'm away? Can you do it for me, Irene?'

She was sobbing as she was led out by a copper who looked as if he might cry too, and I waited until I knew she must have been out of the depressing building before I let my emotions go. I wouldn't cry of course, only Irene had the ability to make that happen. The overriding emotion I had was anger. At myself and at the world. I started to punch fuck out of the cell walls and didn't stop until my knuckles were a mass of mush and blood.

I immediately felt better.

'Come on then, you fuckers!' I shouted through the

door hatch as I bounced around on my toes, fists held in a boxer's stance. 'Sort me transport to me new home then, boys, let's get going!'

Walton Jail in Liverpool was my new home, at least until the High Court hearing when I'd get sentenced. I knew I was going to get time, my solicitor made that clear to me, it was just a matter of how long I'd get. I couldn't tell Irene though, she needed to be told things a little bit at a time, it was all she could take, and she needed a little bit of hope to cling to.

I was the opposite. For me, hope was dangerous and could lead to devastation. Fuck that for a game of soldiers, my motto was to always expect the worst and then anything less than that was a happy bonus.

The jail itself was an old Victorian building that, from a distance, looked a bit like a castle. Inside, however, it was a terrible old place, dilapidated and crumbling, dirty and dismal. In 1974, just 10 years before I got there, the last hanging in Britain had taken place there, and it was said that the corridors and landings were haunted by ghosts of years gone by. Horrible place it was, and I was banged up alone in a cell, left with my own demons, far worse than any fucked up ghost wandering the block.

During the first week I contacted my Mum and arranged for her, Irene and little Michael to come for a visit. I missed them all terribly and I knew Irene must be going out of her mind. I worked hard to get my head straight on the day of the visit, and was determined to be the happy, smiling, joker that they were all used to, but fuck me! The minute I walked into the visitor room and copped for them all sitting at the table, waiting for me, I fucking crumbled, yet again. Jesus Christ, I thought to myself, let's hope I don't get too many fucking years, 'cos I can't be coping with this every visit.

'Daddy! Daddy!' Michael shouted, running towards me. I glanced at one of the guards who nodded it was okay, then I picked my son up and swung him around.

'Come here, my big boy!' I said, happiness bubbling inside of me. 'Oh, I have missed you, my boy.' I kissed him then put my free arm out towards Irene. 'Come here, baby,' I said. 'I've missed you so much, Princess.'

My Mum, bless her, must have been in bits to see me in that dirty visiting block, but to give Mum her due, she gave me a hug and a kiss and then told Irene she'd wait for her outside. She knew we needed time on our own.

'I miss you so much, Mick,' Irene said when she sat back down, leaving Michael on my knee. 'We both do, I just can't cope without you.'

I gazed into her eyes and tried to imprint them into my brain. Those eyes could melt butter just by looking at it.

'I know, baby, I know,' I said, trying to keep my voice level, 'but remember what my brief said, if those fuckers keep schtum, chances are we get a mistrial, or a suspended sentence or something, don't give up hope, baby, I love you so much.'

The idiots I got caught with only had one job. Say fuck all about the shooter. None of us admit to holding it and none of us knew who owned it, it was really that fucking simple. We just had to all of us keep our heads down until the court hearing.

Before we knew it, it was time to say goodbye, and I'm not lying when I say that was by far the hardest goodbye of my life. Young Michael screamed his little head off as Irene had to prise him off me. He had his skinny arms wrapped tightly around my neck and, I'm ashamed to say, I couldn't bring myself to help pull the kid off me. I had to leave it to Irene, who was also crying her heart out.

'Come on, baby,' she pleaded, 'Daddy has to go to work now, we'll see him again soon, I promise.' She yanked him off me, kissed me on the lips and said, 'Just go, Mick, don't make this harder.'

'Daddy! Daddy! I want my Daddy!' Michael screamed hysterically as I walked away.

Within an hour I had smashed my cell to bits, had punched fuck out of my still sore knuckles again, and was thrown into the punishment block for head-butting two screws who came in to calm me down.

My world had started to crumble and there was fuck all I could do about it.

AUTHOR OVERVIEW

IRENE PETERSON

HAD I been assessing Irene around this time, I would have recognised that although she didn't know anything for sure about Mick's criminal activities, she always had an idea that something wasn't quite right. It is my belief that she only allowed herself to dip her toes into the idea that Mick wasn't always doing what he said he was, but then pulled herself back from analysing it any further. She was afraid of actually learning the truth, preferring to remain blissfully unaware.

What Irene was now confronted with was a situation she could never have prepared for given her ignorance about Mick's criminal activities. She faced an uncertain future, possibly as a single mother, and she didn't want it.

FINDINGS

Emotional Turmoil: Irene expressed feelings of confusion, betrayal, and fear. She described her love for Mick but also an intense frustration from his prolonged absences and time spent in the pub. The feelings of anger escalated into heated arguments, which left her feeling isolated.

Denial and Realization: Initially, Irene was in denial about Mick's criminal activities. She had built her life around the idea of a happy family and a loving husband. The police raid marked a significant turning point for her, forcing her to confront the reality of her situation. This realisation has left her feeling lost and questioning her own judgement.

Parental Responsibility: As a mother, her primary concern was the well-being of her toddler. She felt torn between her love for Mick and a fear for the environment he's created for their child. There's a palpable anxiety about the future and what it means for her son.

Support System: Irene indicated a lack of a robust support system. Friends and family were kept at arm's length from the relationship between Irene and Mick, as Irene wanted to be seen as a good wife and mother who could always manage, and so she feels alone in this struggle. The shame and stigma surrounding her situation contribute to her reluctance to reach out for help.

Ongoing Attachment: Despite everything, Irene still felt a strong attachment to Mick. She loved him deeply and believed in his ability to change, which complicated her emotional state and decision-making.

CONCLUSION

Irene was in a challenging position, caught between her love for Mick and the painful truth of his actions. Prior to getting married, Irene had lived a full and happy life, built around solid relationships with her family and friends. She admitted to being the type of person who, in her youth, always believed the grass was greener on the other side of the fence.

In just a few short years she realised that whichever path one took, it was never going to be without complications and challenges. She would now need to find the resilience she had drawn on in the past, to navigate this turbulent time and to empower her to make decisions that prioritise her and her child's well-being.

CHAPTER THIRTEEN

IRENE

IT WAS so traumatic going to visit Mick in that police station after his arrest, but nothing compared to the news that from there, he'd be going to prison on remand. I didn't know what any of it meant, the jargon that Mick and his solicitor used, and I was just so bloody scared.

The next time I saw Mick was when he was on remand in Walton Jail. Mick's Mum, Mike and I went to see him. My first impression of the waiting room there was that it was like a dungeon in a castle. The walls were made out of stone, with a long wooden bench along the side. It was a very scary place and I couldn't bear the thought that Mick had to stay somewhere like this.

From there, we all went into a large canteen-like room which had little tables in it. It reminded me of a cafe I once went to in the market. This was much nicer, I thought, glancing at a little snack bar in the corner, maybe prison isn't so bad after all. Once we were seated, they let the prisoners come in and sit with their visitors. We were allowed to buy tea, pop and snacks for the children. I'm a great tea drinker – there's nothing better than a nice cup of tea – and it always made me smile when Mick called it 'Rosie Lee' or just 'Rosie'.

Mick apologised again and again to me, telling me he loved us both and not to worry as it wouldn't be long before we'd all be back home again together. I had hope – it was what we were all depending on. When it was time to leave at the end of the visit and Mick was whisked away, Mike tried to run after him crying, 'Daddy! Daddy!' It was heartbreaking for all of us.

I was devastated.

October 7, 1974 is a date that would be etched on my brain forever. The most horrific day of my life. I woke up early that morning with a heavy sense of impending doom. I felt sick and didn't want to get out of bed. I didn't want to open my eyes and face the day, yet I knew I must. I had to find strength somehow, if not for me, then for Mick, and for Eira and, most of all, for little Mike, who adored his Dad and needed him home.

This day was the one I had been counting down to, but also dreading, it was the day of sentencing for Mick and I needed to be at Chester Crown Court to pray that the judge sent my Mick home.

'Come on, baby,' I said, smiling at little Mike. He looked so innocent, sleeping in his bed, so happy and comfortable, and I was about to change his world by waking him up today. 'Let's get you dressed, and guess what? After Mummy's ready and we've had breakfast, we're going on the bus to meet Nanny Eira and Aunty Eileen. That'll be nice, won't it?'

Mike sat up and clapped his little hands together, smiling. He was such a happy little soul. 'New truck, Mummy?' he asked, as he hopped out of bed.

'Maybe,' I said, laughing. 'Now come on, sweetheart, let's go have our cornflakes.'

Eira and Eileen were very close, just like all of Mick's family, and I could sense their fear as acutely as my own as we travelled on that dreadful journey to the court. We hardly spoke all the way there other than to answer little Mike's questions, each of us locked in our own thoughts. By the time we got off the bus and were walking through Chester Crown Court grounds, I thought I was going to collapse, my legs were shaking that much.

Looking up at the imposing, old building, it reminded me of a castle, and I wondered just how many battles had been fought within its walls. I glanced around and saw two Black Maria vans. Mick had once told me that they were used to transport prisoners from jails to courts and they had no windows, just bars at the back. I saw this close up now and shuddered as I imagined Mick in the back, looking through the bars and wondering if he'd see the outside world again after today.

'Are you okay, Irene?' Eira asked me as we were shown to a waiting room, 'You look very pale, love.'

Heat seemed to rise suddenly from my toes upwards and I couldn't do anything other than pass Mike to her and run from the room. I found the toilets just in time to be violently sick. I splashed my face and looked in the mirror. Come on, Irene, I told myself, silently, you can do this.

'Sorry, Eira,' I said as I went back to them. 'I needed to be sick, I can't stand this, I'm so scared.'

Eira and Eileen stood up.

'The solicitor's been in for us, love,' Eileen said. 'It's time.'

I stared at the judge in his white wig, he looked so imposing and I was afraid. I looked at the dock, the same dock that a few years previously Myra Hindley and Ian Brady had been standing in waiting to be sentenced. Why is my Mick in that same dock? They were bloody child killers! I thought. My Mick hasn't killed or harmed anyone. I felt like I was in a nightmare, and when the guards brought Mick and his co-defendants up from the cells, I could have cried. I'd heard the solicitor telling Eira that the court cells were the old dungeons, without any heating and each still had the original shackles bolted onto the cold, stone walls. Mick would have hated it.

I felt like I was in a bad dream as I tried to listen to the hearing and the sentencing. The three other defendants – I didn't know them, had never seen them before – had been the ones who'd actually planned the robbery, but they all got short sentences because they'd snitched on Mick as being the one who owned the gun. I heard both Eira and Eileen gasp with horror as Mick was given seven years. I thought I'd heard it wrong. My heart sank as Eira started to cry. I looked frantically towards the dock as Mick was being led away and I caught a glimpse of his face as he tried to look at me. He was as shocked as we were.

'What does run concurrently mean?' I asked the solicitor as he walked over to us, 'I heard the judge say something about that, what does it mean?' I silently pleaded that it was some other way of saying the sentence was to be suspended and that Mick could come home. But I knew I was wrong as the solicitor lowered his head so I couldn't see his face.

'It means he'll serve all of the seven years, Irene,' he said. 'I'm so sorry.'

Seven years! Seven long years that I'd be without my rock, that Mike would be without his Daddy. No more giggling as Mick threw him up onto his shoulders and marched off to the sweet shop. No more little love notes to find in my sugar bowl or under my pillow. My protector, my hero, the love of my life had just been ripped away from me in an instant.

I couldn't be a support to Eira and Eileen right then, I

was too much of an emotional wreck myself, and I had Michael to think about. I hugged them both, lied to them as I reassured them I'd be okay, then got on the bus with my little boy to go home. I cried quietly as the thought hit me that home could never really be home anymore, not without Mick. Little Michael must have sensed the enormity of the situation, because he simply grabbed my hand and cuddled up close to me.

As I got off the bus, back in Sutton, the first thing I saw was the newsagent shop that Mick and his cronies had robbed. As if I needed any more upset, I noticed that the giant billboard outside it had a large sign in it declaring in large letters: LOCAL MAN GETS SEVEN YEARS FOR ROBBERY. It felt like a kick in the teeth and I looked all around me at people going about their business, shopping, laughing, chatting. I wanted to scream at the top of my lungs. How could they all carry on as normal when my life, as I knew it, had been shattered?

I want Mick, I just want Mick! Those words whirled around in my head almost every minute of every day for the next few days as I tried to carry on for the sake of Mike. But even the most basic of everyday tasks, like cooking, cleaning or even just getting a bath were proving to be so difficult. I simply didn't have the strength to try to put on a front and act normally. I couldn't even bear to put the radio on, which I usually loved to listen to because the hit song in the charts then was The Three Degrees,

When Will I See You Again? It seemed like the world was mocking me and I wasn't strong enough to stand up and fight back.

'Come on, Irene, just eat a little bit, love.' My Mum said to me one morning after she'd cooked me some bacon and tomatoes. 'You have to eat, love, or you'll make yourself ill.'

She and my sister had been around most days to check up on me, to make sure I was looking after myself and Michael, but the truth was, I wasn't really. I did all the right things for little Mike of course, washed and dressed him every day, took him out for walks, fed him at the right times, but I was on auto pilot and still in deep shock. I honestly couldn't be bothered to eat most of the time.

'I'm okay, Mum,' I said, pushing the plate to one side, 'and don't worry so much, I do eat when I'm hungry, it's just I've never been to the Social Security office before and I'm a bit nervous.'

Mum sighed and picked my plate up to scrape into the bin.

'I know you are, babbi,' she said, using my Dad's pet name for me. 'That's why our Pauline is going down there with you, she'll help you get the dole money or whatever it is they get and don't be feeling bad about getting it, love, it's there for any of us that hit hard times. You've paid your taxes since leaving school, Irene, you're entitled to it.'

Mum was right about me feeling embarrassed about

putting a claim in for social security, but I had no choice. I'd already taken Michael out of nursery for a while and I was in no fit state to go back to work yet. Without my Mick, I was a lost soul, but I still needed money in order to survive the best I could. I was grateful that my sister was with me because, as we sat waiting our turn in the offices, there was a man sitting opposite us, reading a newspaper. I couldn't believe it when he raised it up and there, splashed all over the front cover was a full page photograph of Mick! I couldn't get up fast enough when my name was called to approach the woman at the desk.

I wouldn't consider myself as a snob, and I had by no means been living the high life with my Mick, but having had the kind of life I'd had with first my parents, and then my husband, it was a huge shock to me to be told the meagre amount I would now be getting to live on. I thought I'd heard her wrong when she stated an amount that would never have even covered the cost of a meal for two at the places I'd dined out in, but no, that was all I was going to get to last me a week and it would only just cover my rent!

I lasted two months before I packed up some clothes for me and little Mike and went back to live with my Mum and Dad. I just couldn't afford to live, eat, clothe us and pay the rent, so I decided that at least if I lived with my parents they would look after us. Then I could use my dole money to keep up with my rent at the house, until I felt able to get myself a job and move back there.

It no longer felt like home and this saddened me, deeply. Every few weeks I would go back to the house, leaving Mike with my Mum, so I could check for post and keep an eye on things, and I gave my next-door neighbour – a young woman with a little girl – my spare key so she could check the house every now and again for me. She'd offered this because she told me she'd seen some undesirables hanging around. Imagine my shock when I went back a couple of months later to find that my 'lovely' neighbour had not only done a moonlight flit – moved out without telling anyone – but she'd helped herself to whatever she'd fancied from my house too! My favourite records, some beautiful glass vases and a gorgeous, red, enamel jug with white daisies on. It sickened me. Talk about hitting someone when they're down!

CHAPTER FOURTEEN

MICK

LANDING AT Walton Jail to serve my sentence was a bit of a shock to the system. I mean, I'd mentally prepared myself for a long stretch, but seven years seemed fucking harsh and was like a lifetime of not having my Irene or my son. I just couldn't get over the fact that I had been ripped away from them and I spent days torturing myself with 'what ifs'. Yes, I'd done some things and yes, I always knew there was a chance I'd be caught and, to be fair, I'd been let off by the courts on more than one occasion when I'd expected to lose my liberty. But to actually lose it for that length of time was a killer and I found I couldn't control the rage that was building inside of me.

Fuck punching walls and hurting myself though, that got me nothing apart from swollen knuckles and an inability to use my fists effectively for a few days and, trust me, you need your fists in a jail like Walton. It was still thought of as a death camp to many because of the hangings that had taken place there and, in 1974, there were still some barbaric fucking screws working there whose only aim seemed to be inflicting misery on those who would take it. Unfortunately for most of them, I was never going to accept any unjust cruelty, taunting or beat downs.

'You think you're fucking hard, do you, Peterson?' One screw screamed at me after two of them had dragged me back to my cell because I'd had a fight in the canteen with two doylems who'd tried their luck with me and lost out.

'Think you can rule the roost, do you, son?' He was waving his baton at me now, grinning and urging his mate to do the same. 'Well, let's see how hard you really are,' he said. 'Fancy taking two of us, do you?'

I grinned back at them. This was the perfect opportunity to de-stress, I thought. 'Come on then, you cunts!' I screamed, holding up my fists. 'Let's have it, boys!'

All hell then broke loose as I ran towards them and they towards me. I was in my element and barely felt the blows raining down on me, the kicks, the batons. In fact, I know without a doubt that I was allowing every single strike and, when I decided to, that's when I let them have it back. To be honest, I was in a blind rage by now, but like many battering routines in the past, I had it down to a fine art and the two screws were soon crawling out of my cell, bloodied and beaten.

'Tah-tah, boys,' I mocked, grinning at them. 'Oh, and

tell the canteen they owe me a jam roly-poly, will you? Never got a fucking chance to finish it, boys.'

I laughed as loudly as I could as they limped away, yelling at me to go fuck myself and warning me this wasn't over, which of course, I knew it wasn't. I'd thrown my cap in the ring now and this meant one of two outcomes. Everyone, screws and inmates, would realise I was no pushover and I'd be left alone, or they'd all realise it, but the screws would now have me down as a trouble causer who needed to be taught a lesson anyway. It didn't take a genius to realise how this would play out, so I had to be ready.

I climbed onto a chair in my cell and managed to see outside. It had started to snow, and it was only at that moment that I realised it was coming up to Christmas. 'Lonely This Christmas', the number one record in the charts that year, popped into my head and I started to sing it, quietly to myself.

My rage subsided as I began to realise this would be the first Christmas I wouldn't spend with my Irene and Michael. Why had I been so fucking stupid? Why had I allowed myself to take such a stupid risk by taking a shooter to a robbery? Poor fucking Irene, poor little Mike. I jumped down from the window as if those snowflakes were taunting me and I rubbed the blood from my face the best I could before throwing myself onto the floor and doing press ups until I was worn out.

I then wrote a long letter to Irene, telling her how much I adored her and how sorry I was that I'd put us all in this situation. Knowing I'd get punished now for my fight, I also explained that to her, because I knew it would affect everything. No way would these fuckers allow me a visit any time soon after this. Which, by the way, had not been any of my doing at all.

I'd been sitting down with my tray, minding my own, when these two Scousers had decided to mock my accent when they heard me speaking to the old guy next to me. I told them nicely to leave it out, but they continued to take the piss. One of them had the nerve to 'accidentally' knock my jam roly-poly off the table, and I stood up to make him pick it up. He and his mate both went for me, so I quickly punched the pair of them in the face. No fuss, no fucking nonsense, and that should have been it, but no, the stupid screws saw it as an opportunity to try to put me in my place.

The next morning, it was two different screws who came to my cell door. One of them looked older than average and he had a nice smile. I jumped off my bunk and started to jump up and down to warm up for the inevitable.

'Two again?' I asked. 'Well, that's fine by me. Not had me brekkie yet, sir, a bit o' screw will do nicely. You brought me a nice cuppa to swill it down with?'

The older of the two smiled.

'Micky, isn't it?' He asked. 'You alright, lad, after

yesterday? Am I alright to come in, lad? No trouble from us, that I can promise you.'

I was a bit taken aback, but I instinctively knew this was a decent man. I couldn't read the other one, who just looked a bit nervous, but I knew that neither was a threat, so I stopped jumping around, lowered my fists and nodded.

'Be my guest,' I said.

'I've worked here for years, Micky, and they all call me Mr B. You'll see a lot of me on this wing, and I think me and you will get along, but you'll have to trust me, lad, okay?'

Trust a screw? Not likely, I thought, but this man didn't snarl like most of them did, and he did seem kind.

'What's the score, then?' I asked. 'Governor's reprimand? Few days in the block?'

The old geezer laughed softly.

'Both of the above, I'm afraid, lad,' he said. Then he looked me in the eyes and asked, 'Can we go see him without any bother, lad? I think it'll just be a couple of days from what I hear. Between me and you, the two officers that set about you never got both sides of the story, now's your chance, lad.'

I smiled at him.

'I'm not grassing, sir, not for no one, but you won't get any bother out of me this morning.'

I ended up doing a week in the block, actually. For one, I refused to speak about the incident because no way would

I grass, and for two, well, I can't keep my fucking mouth shut. There were some right mouthy screws on the punishment block and, me being me, I had to give as good as I got. That resulted in them often 'forgetting' to feed me and when I kicked off, they'd come in mob-handed, sometimes five or six of them, in protective suits and give me a beat down. Ah well, it broke the days up and alleviated the boredom. At night I would lay for hours, filling my head with thoughts of Irene and Michael, hoping that I'd dream about them and wake up happy. I missed them both like crazy.

Mr B turned out to be a diamond of a screw. He was firm but fair, and I learned from others that he'd always been this way and had worked at Walton for many, many years, so he'd seen plenty of executions before all the neck snapping got stopped. I was fascinated by him so, a few weeks later, I was happy to allow him into my cell for a chat and a cup of tea. He had an old-fashioned pipe that he would puff on, and that alone used to make me smile.

'You been in a scrap again, lad?' he asked, as he sipped his tea. 'I see the black eyes are back.'

I laughed and nodded as I reached into my locker for a packet of chocolate biscuits.

'You should see the other fella,' I said, 'and before you ask, I never started it, I just fucking finished it. You know what it's like in here. I'll probably be down the block again by teatime.'

Mr B nodded and said, 'So I've heard, Micky, but you know, lad, they won't ease up on you. I've worked here over 30 years and I know how it goes. You just need to calm it down a bit and things would be easier for you.'

'You know me,' I said, smiling and winking. 'Sweetness and light, me, sir, sweetness and light, me old China.' I sat back down, opposite him. 'Anyway, I hear you were mates with that famous hangman Albert Pierrepoint, and you worked alongside him, is that right?'

'You heard right,' he said. 'In fact, I was one of the death watch screws right here in Walton. I spent many months, weeks and hours with the men who had been sentenced to death and I witnessed more hangings than I care to remember, lad.'

I listened, absolutely silent, as he told me about his time on the death wing. He told me stories about men he'd built up deep relationships with, who he then had to watch being hanged, some of whom he'd put his life on it were innocent.

'Some would go kicking and screaming as that hatch opened up,' he said, with a shudder, 'and then there were those who went down with a smile on their face, relieved to be leaving this life. It was horrible though, in all cases.'

He went on to tell me that Pierrepoint was the most sought after hangman in the country because of his fair and swift way of doing the deed.

'To Albert,' he said, 'it was a nasty job, but someone

had to do it, and as it was him, he wanted to make sure it was fast and as pain-free as possible. He knew other hangmen who were cruel and loved to inflict as much pain as possible and they knew just how to set the noose to ensure it. Evil bastards, some of them.'

I often used to wonder if Albert Pierrepoint ever feared for his own life. I mean, he had a house and a club, I heard. You'd think that some families might have been gunning for him after he'd hanged one of their own, especially if it had turned out they'd been innocent. Mr B told me that did occur quite regularly, as it happened.

Despite all the shit at Walton Jail, despite the shitty conditions and the harsh punishment regime, Mr B was always able to calm me down. Even when I was really riled up, even when the other screws were determined to batter me for some reason or another, I'd only have to listen to Mr B's voice for a few minutes and I felt immediately at ease and able to think straight. He talked me down from many bad situations at that nick, before they shipped me out that is. Too many fights and too many stand-offs saw me getting moved in the middle of the night early in 1975 to Hull Pprison.

Yet another Victorian jail where the conditions were diabolical.

CHAPTER FIFTEEN

IRENE

IT HIT me like a ton of bricks one morning that me and little Mike were truly alone. I'd been trying to make Mike laugh as I did a silly dance to a song playing on the radio and I was chasing him around the kitchen table, pretending to be a monster who wanted to grab him.

'Catch me, Mummy,' he squealed as he set off running in the opposite direction to me, 'Mike dancing too!'

'You are, baby,' I said, 'and what a lovely dancer, you're just like your Daddy, he was a great dancer.'

We carried on for a little while and then the radio DJ announced, '…and next up, we have "Lonely This Christmas" by Mud.'

I was stopped in my tracks and I picked Mike up and held him close into my shoulder so he wouldn't see my tears. I sobbed as the song played and it felt as if the words were mocking me, I couldn't bear it. I just knew that this pain was going to last forever, or at least for seven years and that was forever to me.

The only thing that kept me going was that Mick was a prolific letter writer, and I so looked forward to my twice weekly updates from him. However, as the weeks went by, even that became stressful and I began to recognise a pattern. For every, what I called, good letter, there followed a bad letter, and I'd get really anxious each time I picked up an envelope with his unmistakable handwriting on it. The good letters were so heart-warming, filled with promises for the future. He would write over and over how much he loved me and Mike and how he dreamed of us and pictured coming home. I loved those letters, but the bad ones gave me a sickening feeling that I couldn't shake. These letters must have been written when Mick was angry, because the writing indented the page it was written on and was filled with outrage at the injustice of prison. How he'd lost remission for 'bad behaviour' when all he'd tried to do was stand up for himself or somebody else.

No, Mick, I'd think, you can't win, you're in prison, what do you expect? I never said that when writing back of course. I'd skip over anything he said in his angry letters and fill mine with little tales about Mike and how much we loved him. I made sure never to tell him just how much we were struggling though. That was a burden I didn't want him to have to share.

Mick had bought a car on finance from a man who lived at the top of our road, who had found out about Mick being in prison. He wasted no time in making it clear the repayments still had to be made and would turn up at the door, like clockwork, every week.

'I'm sorry,' I said, one week. 'I'm really trying my best here, but I just don't have the full amount, can I pay you half this week?'

'I suppose you have rent to pay, and bills and such,' the man said, as he leaned against the side of my front door.

'I do, and I'm struggling.' I said, grateful that he seemed to understand.

'Well so do I!' He said with a nasty look on his face, 'and if you fuck me around, then I won't have the money to pay my bills, will I? Look, I'll take half now, and I'll be back in two days for the other half. Best I can do, and make sure you're in when I call.'

With that he strode off down the path, whistling. I hated that bloke and wondered what on earth Mick was thinking of, doing business with a man like that.

Everything was a struggle, and I was loath to borrow money from my parents. In my messed-up brain I figured that it was important to pay the HP payments on my beautiful furniture, but I stopped paying the rent for my house. Madness, on reflection, yet in my unfamiliar, upside-down world I just couldn't prioritise. I cried one morning when I woke up and remembered the dry cleaners still had two of Mick's suits that hadn't been paid for and picked up. I walked, rather than take buses, for a week so that I could go and collect them.

I finally got word from the prison that I could go and visit Mick, and the good news was that they had agreed to send me a discretionary visitor's payment. It was barely enough to pay for the train, but at least it was something. By now, Mick had been moved to Hull Prison, due to his behaviour, so I knew it would be a long journey.

'We'll go with you, love,' Eira said, when I went to take Mike to see them all. 'Me and Joe, and we'll all go on the train. It'll be lovely for little Mike, like a day out.'

'Oh, thank you so much,' I said. 'I was dreading trying to get there by myself, and you're right, Mike will love the train.'

'We'll go into Hull first,' Eira said, 'and get something to eat, some breakfast or lunch depending on what time we get there, and then we'll take you both shopping, love, buy little Mike a nice new outfit to wear to go see his Daddy.'

The day of the visit went exactly as Eira had planned it. After a very long journey, passing some lovely scenery, we finally arrived in Hull. We found a lovely little cafe and all had tea, sandwiches and cake and then went into what looked like a big market, where Joe picked out a gorgeous little outfit for Mike. We got him changed in the bus station toilets while we waited for our bus that would take us directly to the prison gates. On that last leg of the journey, though, I was filled with a feeling of dread. I wasn't sure what it meant, but I was positive something bad was coming, and it scared me.

As at the last prison I'd visited, we were shown to a canteen-like waiting room and were told to take a seat at a table and that Mick would be with us soon. There was a serving hatch along the side where they sold snacks, drinks and sweets etc and a couple of what looked like school gym mats on the floor.

'I think that's where the kiddies can play,' Eira said, after I pointed them out. 'I think that's a box of toys over there, too.'

'Bit of a grim-looking playground,' I said, laughing, and glancing around at the other visitors filling up the seats.

We were all excited and I personally could not wait to see my handsome Mick. I'd pictured this scene in my dreams so many times and I just desperately wanted to feel his arms around me. When he did emerge from the prisoner's door however, I was shocked to see the state of his lovely face. He was covered in lumps and bruises!

'Oh my god, Mick,' I said, bursting into tears. 'What's happened to you? Who did that?'

'Leave it out, Princess,' he said, beaming at me. 'You think I'd let someone do this to me?' He waved his hand around his face and laughed out loud. 'Behave yourself, I walked into a fucking door, now come here, let me look at you and my little baby Mike.'

'He's not a baby anymore,' I laughed as Mick hugged me and then picked Mike up and onto his knee. 'Look at him, he'll be bigger than me soon.'

We had a lovely visit, and it was so nice when this other prisoner came over to our table and tapped Mick on the shoulder. He was holding a bag of sweets and a bottle of pop.

'You alright, Mick?' He asked. 'I hope you don't mind, but I've brought these over for your little lad, is that alright?'

Mick smiled up at the man and patted his back.

'Alright, Charlie. Course it's okay, mate, and thank you, little Mike will love these.' He took the bag and the pop and turned to me.

'This is Charlie Wilson, Irene, a good friend of mine. Here, Mikey, say 'ello to uncle Charlie.'

Mike smiled shyly and allowed the man to pick him up to say hello, it was lovely. When the man went back to his family however, I asked Mick if he was a friend from home.

'Don't you read the papers, Irene?' Mick asked, laughing hysterically. 'It's Charlie Wilson, he's one of the Great Train Robbers.'

The end of the visit came far too quickly, and I was inconsolable as Mick held on to me, kissing my head and trying to calm me down. Right at that moment, I would have stayed in that grotty old grey prison with him.

'Please, Mick,' I said, through my tears as I gazed into his eyes, 'please stop losing your remission, please! And stop fighting with every Tom, Dick and Harry, they'll never let you come home to me. You're going to end up in a mad house.'

'I'll try, baby,' Mick said, winking at me and smiling. 'Now cheer up, don't let our little Mike see you like this.'

It didn't make any difference. Mike was also inconsolable, bless his little heart. I think he thought that this was it, he had his Daddy back, so when he saw him leaving our table with the guards, it took all of my strength to keep him from running after him.

'Daddy!' he screamed. 'Come back, Daddy, come back!'

It was a very quiet train ride home that day, each of us alone in our thoughts, as Mike slept, snuggled onto his Grandad's knee. He was all cried-out for sure, but I knew I wasn't, and I sobbed as quietly as I could as the thoughts swirled around in my head. Just how am I meant to survive seven years of this? I asked myself the question. The emotional hell was far worse than the financial struggles and the day-to-day survival. I'd told Mick he would end up in a mad house, but now I was seriously afraid that I was in danger of losing my own sanity.

CHAPTER SIXTEEN

MICK

HULL PRISON was a fucking shithole. It seemed every bastard and his uncle wanted to have a go at me, including the guards. Every minute of every day I had to watch my back. I saw some proper beatings in that jail, and some proper nasty bastards. God help any poor sod who came in and was a bit effeminate or acted soft. He was set upon by the bully boys almost immediately. Raped, beaten and sometimes even dressed up as a woman, using a ripped up shirt or whatever, and then gang raped. It was hideous for them, but there wasn't a thing they could do to defend themselves. The anger and resentment just built up inside of me, especially after my visit from Irene and Mike. I was raging at the thought of them sitting at home, crying for me.

I was thinking about this one day in the prison workshop and I started to pace.

'Peterson!' This guard shouted. 'Get back to work, it's not fucking Butlins!'

'Fuck off!' I yelled back. 'I ain't fucking working no more in this dump, unless you wanna come make me, screw.'

That was it, as I predicted, the fucker flew at me, blowing his bastard whistle, baton out ready. Everyone else stood back.

'You want some?' I screamed as I charged at him. I absolutely battered him, he never stood a chance against my rage, but then six of the fuckers were on me before I knew it. I only saw the needle as it was being pressed into my thigh and I managed to boot the screw who did it, in his face, before I passed out. I woke up in solitary confinement.

Chlorpromazine or CPZ was what they'd doped me with. When I woke, I was spewing my guts up, violently ill. I'd never felt as bad in my life and thought I was dying. One of the block screws told me it was a knockout drug that they gave to schizophrenics. Fucking charming, I thought, lumping me in with the nutters.

They left me in that block for two months because, apparently, while I was battering the screw, I had smashed up the prison workshop, causing several thousand pounds worth of damage. Good, I thought, no more slave labour for a while. I also got six months added to my original sentence.

I needed to away the time while in there, not just to

keep myself in top fighting form, but to show the screws I wasn't a bit bothered by it, so I started working out. Fast and furious was my MO, and as I did my press ups and exercises for hours on end, every day, I noticed my body changing shape. By the time I went back onto the wing, I had grown muscles on my muscles!

I was always handy at fighting, for as long as I could remember, but with my new fitness regime, I was stronger than ever. I could control, the size of my biceps and my fitness level. Unfortunately, I couldn't control what I did with that once I'd lost my head.

Never in my life have I thought to myself, oh, I think I'll go batter this cunt or that cunt, just for the sake of it. Especially as most men were weaker than me and I'm not a coward. I'd never pick on somebody who wasn't capable of defending themselves. The rage within me was always, always, in my opinion, the result of some injustice. Shitty slop for prison food, convicts being treated like animals and being stripped of their dignity, someone claiming I'd done something when I hadn't, or if I saw bullies hurting someone not right in the head. The only exception were the nonces and beasts. Men who'd hurt little children or had a sexual interest in them. They were sick bastards, and I could quite easily hurt one of them without any provocation. Maybe it's just me, but they deserve to be put down.

My reputation was growing fast amongst the prison

population as somebody who shouldn't be messed with. Unfortunately for me, this also meant that I was to become a victim of my own success. There's a hierarchy in every prison in the country, always has been, always will, and the harder a man is, the higher up the pecking order they sit. All that shit has never been on my radar, I didn't give two fucks about who was 'the daddy' or the 'wing king', I was just me and they could all either take me or leave me, I didn't want or need any embarrassing prison tag. It didn't matter though, because any con who fancied a shot at the title seemed to think that if they put me down, they'd be one step closer. Fucking mugs, the lot of 'em, but it didn't stop them trying.

'Oi, Peterson, you've jumped the fucking queue,' this Leeds lad, called John, said to me one morning as we lined up for breakfast.

I looked at him, puzzled, then looked at the queue, which was only short, and he was about third waiting to be served. I was two behind him.

'Are you off your fucking rocker?' I asked, knowing full well I'd waited my turn. 'Get yer fucking slop and keep yer trap shut, fucking mug.'

I couldn't quite believe my eyes, but he leaned across the counter, grabbed a jug that had once held milk, and came straight at me. He had no chance at all, zero, so fuck knows what he thought he was going to do, but I snatched the jug as he raised it towards me, head butted him and then smashed the jug into his face. He never lifted a finger or threw a single punch, but the fucker would definitely have smashed me with the glass jug, he just wasn't quick enough. You snooze, you lose is what I say. Next minute, I was surrounded by screws yet again. I glanced at that John who was snivelling on a chair by now, and vowed to punish the bastard for this – as I lay on the floor getting booted in the head by five screws, battered in my ribs with their fucking coshes, and then dragged off to solitary.

At least this time they never injected me with that shit they'd used before, so it didn't stop me punching fuck out of as many heads as I could as they threw me into the cell in the block. I'd got two months of it last time, so I expected a lot more than that. They gave me some proper shit down that block, spitting in my food, hosing me down with freezing cold water. One bastard had even collected a load of cockroaches and threw them in my cell. Did they break me? Did they fuck! I laughed at their pathetic attempts to control me, and once again got stuck into my press ups and sit ups. I was determined to give this particular lot of screws a good fight if they tried to come in mob-handed. I worked out all day, every day, so that I'd be able to sleep through the night and dream about my Irene. I took solace in knowing there'd be lovely letters from her, waiting for me when I got back on the wing.

Unfortunately, that never happened. Six weeks into my solitary, I was hauled in front of the governor, charged with assault, got nine months added to my sentence and was told I was getting shipped off to Armley Jail in Leeds. Fucking Leeds! I hoped the cons there were a bit different to that stupid John who I jugged.

As I packed up my kit and waited for a transport screw to collect me, I wrote a letter to Irene. She'd sent a few, and it made me sick to the stomach as I read between the lines and saw how miserable she was without me. It was as if time had stood still for her and, while I was in jail, getting three meals a day, a bed to sleep in, and access to a gym and telly etc without paying a penny for any of it, she was out there, dealing with real life. Bills, rent, feeding and clothing a kid. It killed me to realise I'd done this to her. In the heat of the moment, I started to write, telling her how much I loved her, but that she needed to divorce me so she could move on with her life. Before I had a chance to change my mind, I handed it over for the post and my transport arrived.

CHAPTER SEVENTEEN

IRENE

I'VE HEARD it said that when people get sent to prison, it's hell on earth. They lose everything, including their liberty. Their families are gone, jobs are gone, they're told when to eat, when to sleep and they no longer have access to the things that we, on the outside, take for granted. Over the next couple of years, I learned to ridicule that notion. Life for those left on the outside is hell! It's a lot harder, in my opinion, trying to make ends meet and bringing up a small child alone than being in prison where all the basic needs are taken care of. I never knew where our next pound was coming from and the bills just piled up. I lost our council house as I couldn't get myself out of the accumulating rent arrears and me and Mike ended up living full time at my parent's place.

Time was passing very slowly. I continued to write to Mick and he wrote back, but over two years had passed and we no longer wrote every other day. The letters had dwindled to once a week. I still felt tense though, each time one arrived, and I dreaded reading it if it was going to be a bad letter. Almost every one of them nowadays would include Mick telling me he'd lost more remission, or got more months added on, it was horrible. I began to doubt he'd ever bloody come home. It seemed to me that they all had it in for him because I knew he always acted in self defence, and yet, the visiting court always appeared to believe the 'other guy' and it would be Mick who was punished. I loved him so much, but why was love so painful?

I asked my sister, Jan, that exact question one day when we met for a cup of tea. My Mum had urged me to get out of the house for an hour or two while she looked after little Mike.

'It's not meant to be painful, Irene,' she said, stroking my hand as she spoke. 'I mean, yes, we all have our ups and downs, just look at me and Mike, we've been through it at times, but you and Mick, you are crazy about each other, so it stands to reason that a separation would hurt so much.'

She was right of course. Me and Mick had been obsessed with each other from the start, so of course I would feel separation pain so acutely. It was the price I had to pay for loving so much. Still, that didn't seem fair, and it didn't seem fair that Jan and her husband Mike – who I called big Mike, for obvious reasons – would never understand how badly I was affected by my loss.

'It's awful,' I went on. 'Because I think it feels like he's died and I'll never see him again, only he hasn't, he's right here. The letters prove that, but he's just out of reach and me and little Mike are living a life he can't be part of. It's hard to explain.'

'Listen, Irene,' Jan said. 'I do understand, honestly, but Mike and I were talking, and we see how you're being swallowed up. You're drowning in grief and it's not good for you or little Mike. I know Mick would agree with us, he'd want you to be happy, lovey, you know this. We'd both like you to come and stay with us for a couple of days. Leave the little fellow with Mum and Dad, and just take a break from everything while we make some plans for going forwards.'

I didn't have to think about the invitation for too long and, a couple of days later my brother-in-law, big Mike, collected me in his car and we were soon pulling up on the drive of their brand new bungalow on the outskirts of Helsby. They'd built the bungalow themselves and it was huge. It felt like I was on my holidays. It was beautiful, inside and out. The day after I arrived, big Mike came home just as me and Jan were making tea together and laughing about the old days, when we were children. He was waving an envelope in front of my sister.

'I know you told me to cancel this,' he said, 'and I did

try to, I explained we had family staying and couldn't go, but I'm afraid you'll have to dig out another ball gown, darling, because they've given me an extra invite for Irene, so we're going after all.'

I was confused, but Jan explained that they'd been invited to a policeman's ball. Big Mike used to have an important job on the council and had all kinds of connections, the police being one of them.

'Oh, say you'll come, Irene,' Jan pleaded. 'It's tomorrow night, these things are so much fun, and you never know, you might even meet a lovely policeman to take you out for dates.'

I raised my eyebrows at that. I could imagine Mick's reaction, him a prisoner and me out gallivanting with a police officer. Still, I knew my sister meant no harm.

'It will be fun,' I said, smiling, 'and it's about time I started getting out and about again, let's do it.'

We even had fun trying on my sister's fancy dresses, but in the end I opted for high fashion, as always. I did love the colours and styles of the 70s. I wore a brightly coloured dress and tied a long, matching scarf around my forehead, and it got me loads of attention. I knew I looked good, and I felt good, too. There were lots of eligible, good-looking men at that ball and a few of them wanted me to go out with them, but I politely declined. I was still in love with my Mick.

Although I chatted and laughed with men and women

that night, I wasn't entirely closed to the idea of dating anybody, it was just too soon.

That night out was the start of my new journey as a single mum. I had to accept that this was me now, a wife without a husband, a mother without a present father figure for her son. Something had to change if I was to get back to my old self, and it would start with me finding a job. Goodness knows why I decided to set my skills as a typist aside and look for a bar job, but that's what I did. I had started to think about my old friends and how much I missed going out and having fun, so I figured working behind a bar would be the next best thing, and at least I'd meet new people. I browsed the local paper and found the perfect job to apply for. A bar server was required for a huge hotel that was really close to my parents' house. I knew the hotel, it had a large bar area and a nightclub downstairs. I applied straight away and was offered the job immediately.

My first shift was on a Saturday night, their busiest night of the week, and I was so flustered. I kept making mistakes and mixing up orders. Any time I received a tip or had a drink bought for myself, I was too embarrassed to accept it, so I simply rang it in the till, tips as well! All the other staff would come away with quite a bit of money at the end of each shift, not me though, I only got my wages. I decided that me and bar work weren't meant for each other. I did stick it out, though and, despite my reservations, I enjoyed the odd night out with a male companion. Nothing serious, really, just somebody to go out and dance with and have a few drinks with. It made me acknowledge that perhaps I might be open to the idea of dating again. But still hadn't really met anyone who was like me; a new best friend.

'I've got an idea,' Mum said one evening after I'd been moaning about always working and never going out. 'I was reading the *Liverpool Echo* today and do you know they have a column where people reach out to meet others? I looked through it, there's loads of people just like you looking for a pal.'

I laughed. 'Mum! That's the dating column,' I said. 'It's men looking for women or the other way around. I'm not looking through that.'

'You're wrong, Irene,' Mum said. 'I've gone through it, and there are quite a few girls advertising for a friend to go out for drinks with. Girls that are new to the area or have come out of a relationship or something and want to meet friends, you should take a look.'

Mum was right! I read all through the column she'd mentioned and I kept being drawn to an advert from a young woman called Trish. She had just moved to the area and was looking to meet friends to go out for meals and drinks with. She sounded really nice, so I answered her ad. I was so pleased I did as the very first night we met up, we got along like a house on fire! She was very pretty, owned a lovely little car and had the same sense of humour as me. We had a real laugh and she made me feel like I'd been missing out on so much fun for the last few years.

I decided to quit my job the very next day. My boss was fine about it and didn't mind that me and Trish still went in there drinking after I left. It was a fun place to be after all, especially on the party side of the bar.

A couple of weeks later I received a letter from Mick telling me that I should divorce him. He told me I needed to start living my life without him, as he'd been given even more time on his sentence and he felt it was unfair to expect me to wait around. I was devastated, because actually, I had started to live again. And even though Mick's parents had said a couple of times that maybe I should divorce him, because it didn't seem like he even wanted to get out, always getting into trouble inside. But for me, it had never been any more than a fleeting thought. I immediately wrote back and told him absolutely not, I loved him with all my heart and that was the end of the matter.

CHAPTER EIGHTEEN

MICK

ARMLEY JAIL in Leeds opened my eyes a bit, not because it was any worse than any of the others, but it was the first time I was introduced to the strong boxes.

It seemed my violent reputation had preceded me, because as soon as I got there, I was shackled and told I was being taken down to the dungeon. I wasn't afraid, and I assumed 'dungeon' was Armley speak for solitary confinement or something, so I just grinned at the screws taking me down and told them I could do with a nice rest. I was surprised, however, to find that it was in fact an old castle dungeon they were taking me down to, cold and dark and I could smell the damp as we got closer to my new home. We came to a stop outside what I can only describe as the smallest, most secure, bleak cell I'd ever seen.

'What the fuck's this?' I asked as the little fat screw

unlocked a big steel door, only to be met with another steel door that had a small, grated hatch about halfway up it.

'It's your hotel room, Micky,' the taller of the two replied. 'Room service is a bit shit like, but you'll get used to it. We've been waiting for you.'

'Strip off,' the little fat one said as they pushed me inside, still shackled. 'We'll help if you need it.'

'Strip off?' I shouted. 'You a fucking poofter or something? I ain't stripping off, and you best keep the fuck away from me if you know what's good for you.'

I don't know what I thought I could do in shackles, but believe me, I did my best. They came at me, tearing my baggy prison kit off, but I nutted each of them in turn, almost laughing because they weren't expecting it and had no protective gear on. I even managed to use my knees on them too after they got me to the ground. It was hardly a fair fight though, two of them against a chained-up man, but I managed to hurt them enough that they screamed at me that my two days had now turned into a week. Naked, battered and bruised, I was thrown across the room as they ran out, locking the two steel doors behind them.

As my eyes adjusted to the bright striplight, I was able to properly take in my surroundings. The first thing I noticed was that there was no fucking bed. A rectangular shaped board, embedded into concrete with a blanket folded at one end of it was what I was expected to sleep on. No mattress, no pillow, just one poxy, rough-as-fuck blanket. The walls were all concrete and there was no window, no fucking toilet either, just a big pot that I'd have to shit and piss in. I had no doubt that, like the screw had said, room service would be shit in this particular establishment.

By now I had perfected the art of keeping my mind and body active while being isolated, and in this place I had no choice. They left the bright striplight on at all times, so I had no clue of time. The only measure I had was when meals got shoved through the hatch, but I didn't even trust that, I was convinced the screws were fucking with my head and bringing me breakfast at night and tea in the morning, I had no idea. In any case, I only slept when my body was exhausted, which was often, because it was freezing in that fucking concrete coffin and the only way to warm up slightly was to pace up and down for hours in the tiny box cell.

Nobody came to talk to me, ever, even when passing food through, and I knew it was a cruel ploy to try to break me. A lesser man would have gone mad in there, and many have, it was like a torture chamber and the constant buzz of the striplight, along with the steady drip, drip, drip of water from condensation falling to the floor was almost enough to drive me insane.

Almost. Determination to beat the system was what kept me balanced and I was able to get into a routine, even there. I would relive nights out with Irene as I lay on the cold, hard floor, smiling as the images filled my head. I refused to allow myself to think about asking her for a divorce and told myself that when I got out of here I'd have a lovely letter waiting, telling me not to be daft and filled with little stories about what our Mike had been getting up to. I remembered striding down to the newsagents with Mike on my shoulders and people stopping me in the street to tell me what a lovely boy he was, and then taking him to the park. I could clearly hear Irene's soft giggle and Mike's laughter in my head and I would go to sleep happy, despite my surroundings.

They'd never fucking break me.

I got out of the strong box after a week and was put into general population on the wing where, once again, I was confronted by cons who'd already heard all about me from the bent up screws. I fought my way through the next six months, angry because I'd promised Irene I would stop fighting the inmates and the system when she refused to divorce me.

After every fight, I'd be thrown back into the boxes, but now I was used to them, so when they were releasing me, I'd go straight into attack mode because the fights had never been of my own making and I was livid. I'd get a full-on beating with the usual batons, boots and fists before being thrown straight back in. It was a vicious cycle that I wouldn't back down from.

'Peterson!' I heard through the hatch one day. It shook

me up a bit because I hadn't heard a human voice for at least a fortnight.

'The fuck do you want?' I shouted back.

'Time to go, son,' the voice shouted back. 'But there's six of us out here, so no nonsense when we open the door, alright? You're being shipped out.'

I cocked my head to one side and thought about it.

'Shipped out where?' I asked. 'Best not be that fucking Hull or Wakefield, I'm sick of these fucking northern shitholes.'

'Back where you come from, cockney land, mate,' another voice shouted with a pathetic attempt to mimic my accent. 'You coming out the easy way, or what?'

'Open the fucking doors then,' I said, smiling to myself. Much as I wanted to show these six the result of the 200 press ups I'd already done that day, I'd skip the scrapping if it meant I'd be moved down south and away from this hell hole. They didn't make it easy however, even though I showed no resistance. I was dragged out and into another room where I was told to dress in the overalls provided and then I was shackled to be taken to the van that would transport me. I was about to relax a bit, until they opened the back doors of the van up and I saw another four guards waiting inside it for me. Not normal carry on at all.

'What's all this, then?' I asked, snarling at them so they knew I was ready to pounce if they wanted a rumble. 'How many of you does it fucking take?'

'On the floor, Peterson,' one of them said, 'belly down.'

I had no choice as the six that had escorted me pushed me forwards and pinned me down. I couldn't believe my fucking eyes when I saw the chains. They actually chained me to the floor of the van to travel all the way to Wandsworth Jail in London. Not the most comfortable journey I've had in my fucking life.

Half a day later, and just when I thought I was going to get comfortable, they hauled me out of the van, frogmarched me in through the giant wooden and iron gates of Wandsworth into the reception area to book me in. After all the usual procedure of kit and taking down particulars, I was told, 'Straight to solitary confinement, one month.'

What a fucking liberty.

A month down the block saw me working out like never before. I needed to do it to control my rage at the injustice of my life in prison. The guards went for me, I hit back. The inmates wanted a go to further their reputation, I hit back. The bully boys and rapists attacked the weak, I hit back. Our human rights were held back from us on a daily basis, I rioted against the regime. I never started out as a bully, or a killer, or a maniac or an activist, but prison and all it stood for was systematically moulding me into what they liked to say I was. I was so angry and this time I couldn't hold back. I was huge by the time I came out of solitary and was put on the wing and, can you believe it, I was padded up next door to a proper wrong 'un. Just my luck. And to top it all, there were no letters waiting for me from my Irene, so I could only assume that she was losing faith in me, or that the prison officials were holding back my mail. I chose to believe it was the officials, they would do anything to torment me.

After three weeks of not receiving anything at all, I was raging. I didn't want to batter any screws and get put into isolation again, although compared to Hull and Wakefield's blocks, this one was a piece of piss, and quite comfortable, really. I also didn't have the hassle of anyone trying to climb the prison social ladder by attacking me because, by now, I was a huge mass of muscle and I'd have torn them to pieces. I had to get my frustration and anger out somehow though, so I did the next best thing, I tried to poison the fucker in the cell next to me.

The bloke was called Si Si, and oh, he did my fucking head in! Always shouting his mouth off, threats and shit that he could never follow through. I'd scream at him to shut the fuck up, but he just wouldn't listen. I got it into my head that the only way to stop him would be to fuck his throat up so he couldn't shout anymore. I got hold of some glass, crushed it up in my cell, then mixed it with sugar – which was very scarce in there at the time. I then made sure the bag of sugar would find its way to Si Si's cell. Job done. I heard him screaming out the next day and he was taken off to the infirmary.

Parkhurst prison on the Isle of Wight was my next destination, thanks to that little stunt. So, yet again, I was on the move. After going through intake, I was fucking fuming to find out I was going straight to their strong boxes. Filled with dread, not fear, I tried to mentally prepare myself as I was once again shackled up and led down.

I knew Parkhurst was one of the country's few maximum-security jails, so I was guessing my experience might be worse than it had been in the Yorkshire jails. It was very similar, but not worse. I still got the strip down treatment and the accidental elbow to my face and ribs, but after the screws backed out and locked the door, I could see that at least there was something to put on. A horrible, scratchy outfit that didn't fit me anyway, as it happened. I remained naked. This time, there was also a type of fan heater, high up on the wall. I was suspicious about it and I was right to be. The box went from freezing cold, to boiling hot for hours on end, and it was all down to the screws who controlled it, they made it almost impossible to sleep. The screws here used to keep watch on us, too. Silently looking through the hatch to see if their cruelty was having the desired effect. This only made me more determined of course. I would do thousands of press ups and sit ups, I'd sing at the top of my voice and I'd lay down on the concrete, with my back turned as if I were having the best sleep of my life.

I eventually got out, of course, and was leaping up

and down, fists up and smiling as they opened the doors, standing there in riot gear.

'What's up, lads?' I asked. 'Beautiful day for a stroll, isn't it?'

They all looked at each other as if they thought I was mad. 'You've got one chance, Peterson,' one of them said. 'Come out nicely or you'll be thrown straight back in. Governor's orders. So, what's it gonna be?'

'Behave, you silly fuckers,' I said, laughing. 'Sweetness and light, me, mate, sweetness and light.'

I was delighted to find that on my wing were the Kray brothers, Ronnie and Reggie. I knew all about them, of course, and I'd always been interested in their previous boxing history. I loved boxing, my Dad had been a champion boxer when he was in the navy, Smokin' Joe Peterson he was known as, and he had been serving with his good friend, Randolph Turpin, who I knew as Randy. He ended up being a world champion. I introduced myself to the Krays straight away and we got along immediately, we became really good pals.

'Course we've heard of Randy Turpin,' Reggie said, when I spoke about it. 'Proper old school boxer he was, mate. Size of you, Micky, you should start doing it professionally when you get out.'

'It's something to think about,' I said. 'But don't you need a licence to go pro? I dunno if I'd get one with my record, lads.'

'You get yourself down the gym every day, son,' Ronnie said. 'Learn some discipline, and leave the rest to us. We have contacts in boxing, we can get you hooked up.'

I actually really loved it in Parkhurst. Me and the Krays became firm friends and it was so good hearing lots of familiar accents. The only downside was that it was really far to travel down to for my Irene, Mike, and my parents. I had at last received a letter from my Princess, but it had made me sad, as I could tell she was getting bored of the solitary lifestyle I'd left her with. I knew the feeling! Despite the letter not being filled with all of Irene's usual humour and love, I wrote straight back to assure her she was still the love of my life. It put a spring in my step and I was happy to be alive, so imagine my dilemma when this bastard of a screw decided he had it in for me. Couldn't keep his fucking trap shut every time he saw me, and it was becoming embarrassing in front of the other cons. In the end, I had to have a word. I walled him up and got myself nose to nose with the ugly bastard and told him I'd kill him if he didn't fuck off out of my face every day. That's all it took! I was dragged off to the block and shipped back to Wandsworth the next day.

Within a month, I got the idea into my head that I'd escape. It seemed that no matter what I did or didn't do, the system was determined to keep me inside by one means or another and I was sick of it. I started to dig my way out of my cell using a tool I'd sneaked out of the workshop. Every night I'd be at it, scraping the wall, and then covering it up with bricks I'd saved. The dust and mess all went down the bog, and it was enough to keep my head straight and my anger at bay.

But just two weeks in, some muggy bastard grassed me up and once again I was dragged off to solitary confinement, this time for four months. My rage was at boiling point for this, not so much the solitary, I was used to that, but at the fact that I'd been grassed. That is something you just do not do in jail, everyone knows that.

The press-ups didn't seem to be working and I ended up yanking my bed from its bolts and using that as a weight to exercise with. That, of course, brought the screws in, and before they managed to pin me down, I ended up battering two of them. I got a proper kicking for that and was left snotted up, bleeding and barely able to move. Then, to add salt to my wounds, two days later, while I was still recovering, a screw opened the hatch and threw a large envelope at me as I lay, curled up on the floor.

'Here, big lad, even your fucking wife doesn't want you!'

It was signed divorce papers from my Irene. I simply couldn't take it in and I was too rough to even think about it. All I could think was, my life is over, I have nothing left to live for. When the pen came flying through the hatch and the screw shouted that he was waiting for it back, I simply signed each page and stuffed them and the pen back through at the screw.

'Fuck you, you cunt,' I said, with all the bravado I could muster.

The minute I was taken back upstairs, I found the fucker who had grassed me up and gave him the biggest beating of his life. I no longer cared what would happen to me and was expecting to be taken straight back down the block. Instead, I was escorted to the governor.

'I want you out of here, Peterson,' he said, 'and believe me, I've been trying to get rid of you since the minute you landed here, but the only place that will accept you is C-wing, back at Parkhurst.'

'The fucking nutters wing?' I asked, outraged at the thought.

'The psychiatric wing, yes,' the governor said, nodding. He then looked at the four screws who'd brought me to him. 'Is the transport ready?'

'I'm going now?' I yelled. 'That prick had it coming, why the nutter wing? Why not just the block there?'

'They're sick of you, too, Peterson,' he said.

With that I was dragged out, putting up the best fight I could, given the situation, and I was ghosted off to the Isle of Wight again, though not to my mates in general population, but to the nonces and the basket cases.

I wouldn't be standing for that for very long.

AUTHOR'S OVERVIEW

Mick faced significant emotional turmoil since his incarceration for armed robbery, particularly with the separation from his wife, Irene, and their young son, Mike. This second retrospective report outlines Mick's progress and addresses his psychological challenges.

IMPROVEMENTS:

Self-Reflection: Mick showed moments of insight, usually during his periods of isolation, during which he recognised the impact of his actions on his family. He expressed guilt and sadness over hurting Irene, especially after seeing her show physical signs of distress during visits.

Communication with Irene: Although Mick's letters fluctuate between love and rage, there is a clear effort to maintain a connection with his family. He has begun to articulate his feelings more clearly in his letters, acknowledging his struggles and the continuing love he has for Irene and Mike.

Understanding Consequences: Mick is becoming more

aware of the long-term effects of his aggressive behaviour. During communication with Irene, in person and through letters, he has started to express a desire to break the cycle of violence, realising that his actions not only affect him but also harm his family and some of his fellow inmates.

CHALLENGES:

Aggression and Violence: Mick continues to engage in physical altercations, both with inmates and prison staff. His strong sense of justice compels him to defend those he perceives as vulnerable, leading him to confrontations that escalate into violence. This behaviour has resulted in extended time in solitary confinement and additional charges, adding time onto his original sentence.

Isolation: Currently in the psychiatric wing of a maximum-security facility, Mick's isolation has exacerbated his feelings of abandonment and anger. The receipt of divorce papers from Irene has intensified his emotional distress, leading to thoughts of revenge and further violent outbursts.

Resistance to Authority: Mick exhibits a significant level of distrust toward the prison system, viewing it as a punitive environment that seeks to break him. His belief that he is an activist fighting for inmate rights often leads to confrontations, resulting in further isolation.

CHAPTER NINETEEN

IRENE

I WAS still going out and having fun with Trish and we met lots of new friends. My social life was certainly expanding and I began to love life again. I found the fun Irene once more and everybody benefitted from it. Little Mike was happy, my Mum and Dad were happy. In fact, the only downside was that nagging doubt in the back of my mind. Was I being fair to either Mick or myself? I knew exactly what I was doing, I couldn't bear to cut ties with Mick even though I knew I should. My parents thought so, my friends thought so, bloody hell, even Mick's parents had once said as much to me, so why hadn't I?

'Just write him a letter, for god's sake,' Trish said one night when we were driving in her car to a new club in Manchester. 'I know you still write to him, just tell him, Irene, that it's time for that divorce he asked for.'

'That was bloody two years ago,' I said. 'He didn't mean it, he thought he was doing the right thing for me.'

'He *was!*' Trish said. 'And look, it doesn't matter if it wasn't the right time back then, the truth is, it is now, and you know it, Irene. Look how happy your Mike is, look how happy you are! If you ask me, I think you're keeping Mick there in the background just because it's comfortable having him there and you're afraid if you let him go, everything you've built up without him will start to crumble away. That's my opinion.'

I stared at Trish, her words really hitting home, and I realised she was right. Mick had always been my comfort blanket, my safe space, my protector. But I was a grown woman with a son who needed me to be his protector. All this time I had been allowing myself to think that I'd been going it alone, when the truth was that while I still had Mick in the background, I'd never really been alone at all.

'Not only that,' Trish went on, her eyes still on the road, 'but you're still tarnished with his name, Irene, and I don't mean that in a bad way really, I just mean that while you're still married to him, what kind of man do you think would ever be completely comfortable dating you? The wife of Mick Peterson? They'd have to be certifiably mad themselves!'

I laughed out loud, Trish had such a way with words, but the reality was that she was right. Again. There'd been many times over the last couple of years that I'd been having a laugh with Trish or some other friend and a couple of guys, then I'd happen to mention who my husband was and suddenly they had to get going for some reason or another. Had I subconsciously been using Mick as a reason not to get close to anybody else? The answer was clear, that's exactly what I'd been doing.

The following Monday I went to a solicitor and filed for a divorce. I was told that I'd get copies of everything in the post and Mick would be served with papers to sign, then I'd get a date for the court hearing and it would all get finalised.

As I walked away from the solicitor's office, it felt weird. I had a sad feeling because I knew I'd never love anyone like I loved Mick, yet I'd done what was right for me and our Mike. I'd finally taken that last step towards becoming a woman who would stand on her own feet again. It was quite liberating and, for the first time in a long time, I was excited about the future.

'Well done, my love,' Mum said when I got back home. Mike was at school and Dad was pottering in the garden. 'It's for the best you know, me and your Dad have been worrying about you, Irene.'

'Well, I've done it now, Mum,' I said as I chewed on my lip, wondering how to tell her what else I'd done. 'And, Mum,' I said. 'I also got the solicitor to send Mick papers to sign to say that he will have nothing more to do with our Mike, he deserves a fresh start too.'

'What?' Mum said, looking bewildered. 'You can't do that, Irene, he's the boy's father, no matter what he's done.'

I took a deep breath in.

'Well I've done it and that's that. I can't continue taking Mike to see him, Mum, I just can't. And before you say it, I can't have Joe and Eira taking him either. He'll still come home upset and with tales of Mick, I just think it's best to cut ties completely. After all, the way Mick's going, poor bloody Mike will be a teenager before his Dad gets out. I want a better life than prison visits and letters for him, Mum.'

I think that although Mum said she understood in the end, she honestly didn't, and it upset her for a long time. She respected my wishes however, and both she and Dad stopped bringing Mick up in conversations around Mike and I.

Mum also knew that I'd struggle to tell Eira and Joe about my decisions, so she told them for me. They weren't happy, and said they still wanted to see Mike, but they'd prefer Mum to take him to them. It saddened me because I'd always had a beautiful relationship with them both and I knew now it was over for good.

I finally felt like I could go out, guilt free, and enjoy life again. That's exactly what I did and, within a year, I was going out regularly with Dave, who I'd bumped into one night while out with Trish. He was a local lad, but had spent years travelling around Australia.

'I love you, Irene,' he told me one night as we watched a movie at his place. 'Let's get married.'

I didn't have to think about it, really. I was definitely ready to settle down and give up the partying again.

'Are you sure?' I asked. 'It's just that, me and Mike come as a package, you get that, right?'

'Of course I do,' Dave said, 'and we'll have a couple of kids of our own. We'll be a perfect family.'

That's all I needed to hear and within days we were booking our wedding at Birkenhead register office and I was hunting down a wedding dress.

I've always been a bargain hunter, so I was thrilled when I found a long, cream, maxi dress in Birkenhead market. I bought it to get married in, then saw a lovely handbag which matched it perfectly, but I couldn't afford it. I strolled around the market looking for something cheaper, but then it hit me. I could pawn the wedding ring that Mick had bought me. I felt a pang of guilt, but I hurried to the local pawn shop before I could change my mind. I had the ring with me. For some reason I'd always carried it around in my bag, so I fished out my beautiful, white gold wedding ring and handed it over to the jeweller. He only offered me £3 for it, but that was the exact price of the lovely cream handbag I wanted, so I accepted and rushed back to the stall. It seemed like a sign to me that Mick was okay about me starting a new life with Dave.

'I'm pregnant,' I announced to Dave just a week later.

'I can't believe it, I thought we were being careful. What am I going to tell Mike? Oh my god, what will Mum and Dad say?'

Dave stared at me for a moment and then smiled.

'Well, that's okay, Irene, we can get married sooner and we always planned to have a baby anyway, it's fine. Your parents will be fine and, as for Mike, well, he will get used to it. You and him need to stop living in the past, it's our future now – yours and mine. Stop worrying.'

I tried to put it to the back of my mind and, like Dave suggested, I concentrated on the here and now, but things were never that straightforward for me. When I rang the register office I was shocked to be told that not only could I not bring the wedding forward, but I couldn't have the day I'd already booked, either. My Decree Absolute hadn't come through to me and I wasn't allowed to remarry without it.

I really didn't want to tell Dave about this, because something about the way he spoke whenever I mentioned Mick made me feel uncomfortable. There had been a long postal strike and apparently a few people were having the same problem. I was frantic.

'What am I going to do, Dad?' I pleaded, when I got home. 'I'm here, pregnant, and now I'm scared to tell Dave the wedding's being put back, not brought forward!'

'Don't you worry, babbi,' he said. 'Leave it to me. I'll get on to the court and solicitor, and I'll phone Dave to tell

174

him we want the wedding in a month or so, it'll be sorted by then. I'll say it's because some family will be on holiday or something.'

Whatever Dad said, Dave was fine about it and I finally got my hands on my paperwork and was able to book a new wedding date, so everything went ahead and we had a lovely reception at my parent's house. Mum had booked a professional photographer and there was a piece and photograph of Dave and I in a local magazine, *Cheshire Life*. All in all, it was a very different occasion to my first wedding and I felt very special. The only fly in the ointment was that Mike really did not like Dave right from the off and he wasn't happy about the wedding at all. I was determined that I'd change that, though, and told myself that in time Mike would accept Dave as his new Dad and that it would get easier once the new baby came along.

I learned very quickly that hopes and wishes weren't enough to make things so.

'Get away from my Mummy!' Mike shouted to Dave one evening when we were sitting together watching the soaps. Me and Dave were side by side and Dave had his arm around my shoulders.

'Mike!' I said. 'It's okay, baby, you come sit on the sofa with us.'

'No,' said Dave, 'and he's not a baby, Irene, he has to get used to the fact that you're my wife, not just his Mum, and he's not the only child in this house any more.'

We had a baby girl, Leicia. She was so beautiful and the apple of Dave's eye. I couldn't help notice, though, that the love on his face for Leicia, simply wasn't there when he looked at Mike. I saw that he tried, he really did, but I suppose genes win out in the end.

I felt that my loyalties were being tested over the next couple of years and, as a mum, I was always more protective of my boy. Dave hated that, but I always pointed out that I did everything I could to make things easier for him. I'd even stopped Mike from seeing his paternal grandparents. He'd stopped talking about Mick for over a year now, and I was afraid that being with Eira and Joe would be too painful for him, or that they might sneak him on a visit with them, so I did the unthinkable and stopped all contact. A choice I would deeply regret forever.

On the surface, my life looked lovely. I had two beautiful children, a hardworking husband, a gorgeous house and everything I wanted. Underneath, however, I was on edge and always felt that something was missing. A bit like I used to feel years ago, when I was a teenager.

My OCD was back with a vengeance too, but this time it was much worse, and my routines were enough to drive me mad, so it must have been bad for those witnessing it. I had strange compulsions like standing up and sitting back down 20 times and then having to do it all over again if I lost count or somebody distracted me. I'd been seeing things in the newspaper a lot recently about Mick, so I did wonder if that had caused it. According to the papers he was responsible for some prison riots and he was practically a raving lunatic now, beating people up and almost killing them. One headline even likened him to Hannibal Lecter. It didn't sound like my Mick at all, but it did frighten me.

'Irene, Irene!' Dave was calling me and shaking my arm as I tried to wake up one morning.

'Mick?' I said, rubbing my eyes. Then, realising what I'd said, 'Sorry, Dave,' I went on, 'it was just a bad dream.'

'Dreaming about *him* were you?' Dave asked, slamming my cup of tea onto the bedside table. 'You're my wife, Irene, you need to stop buying the bloody papers if you can't help checking in on him.'

I'd actually been dreaming that I was in prison and that I'd tried to escape, but all the inmates had been chasing me to prevent me climbing the wall. It was really scary and I didn't know what it meant, but I did stop buying newspapers after that. I didn't stop reading them though. Dad always saved his for me to read when I went round to theirs, but he was always careful to tear out any pages that had stories about Mick in them.

'Just in case the lad happens to pick them up,' he said, after I'd noticed. 'Best he doesn't know any of that carry on.'

So, I had both my parents and Dave acting as though Mick had never existed. But as hard as I tried, there wasn't a day when I didn't think about him. It didn't help that as Mike got bigger, he was the spitting image of his Dad. Every time I looked into his beautiful eyes, all I could see was Mick. My Leicia, as she started to grow into herself, looked like me when I was little, but not Mike, there was no mistaking where he came from and it made me happy. Even though Mike never really bonded with Dave, he did like his Dad. I think he saw him more of a father figure, to be honest and, one day, when Mike was eight years old, Dave's Dad called to take him for a walk to the park and the sweet shop. I decided to make the most of my free hour and turned on the TV to watch while I tidied up in the living room.

'Our reporters have exclusive access to Broadmoor hospital for the criminally insane,' the news reporter was saying as she stood outside the prison gates. I sat on the sofa, mesmerised as I'd heard that Mick was being sent there. The cameras then moved to the inside of Broadmoor and suddenly my heart leapt into my mouth. There was Mick, walking down a long corridor as a reporter was speaking. I had no idea what was being said, I was simply transfixed, watching the man walking. It was the back of him in the shot, but he was speaking and I recognised his voice immediately, and his walk. I couldn't take my eyes off the screen until the cameras left and it was the outdoor news reporter again. It really unsettled me, but also upset me that Mick really was in such a place. Why can't you forget, Irene? I asked

myself, but how could I? Mick was everywhere I turned. The papers, the TV and in his son. I was destined to never forget my first love.

The next time I saw Mick on the television, it was a news broadcast again, once more, it was filmed at Broadmoor hospital. This time I really couldn't believe my eyes and I was at my Mum and Dad's house when the news came on:

Prolific offender and the man known as Britain's most violent criminal is currently staging a rooftop protest at one of the country's most secure hospitals. According to sources in Broadmoor, Michael Peterson is protesting against treatment he is receiving while being incarcerated here and is refusing to come down from the roof until his demands are met. It's unclear what those demands are at the moment, but Peterson has already caused thousands of pounds worth of damage.

'Daft sod,' my Dad said as he jumped up to change the channel. 'Good job our Mike wasn't with you to see that, eh?' He tried to make a joke out of it then, 'I tell you what, babbi, all that climbing chimneys when he was working came in handy for this malarkey!'

I laughed along with Dad, but my nerves were shot. Poor bloody Mick, I couldn't believe the mess he'd got himself into. I remembered vividly the time I'd warned him he'd end up in a nut house if he didn't behave and silently pleaded that what I'd done – cutting him off and remarrying to Dave – had nothing to do with his current situation.

CHAPTER TWENTY

MICK

THE C Unit at Parkhurst was diabolical, filled with full-blown lunatics and not one person I had anything in common with. I wanted to be on the normal wing, but nobody would listen, even when I explained that I'd be unable to keep my head down, walking around with a wing full of nutcases. I was in and out of the strong box like a fucking yo-yo, because the thing about loonies is that they have no fear, no moral compass, and no filter. They didn't seem to understand that saying the wrong thing to me, or attempting to hit me, would result in them getting hurt, and that's what was happening on a daily basis.

The one saving grace was a screw called Mr Connell. I had a lot of respect for him because he understood me and would try to talk me down when I was raging. The others didn't give two fucks, but Mr Connell never gave up on me and he'd be the one to come meet me when I was getting released from a strong box.

'You got it this time, Mick,' he'd say. 'You can do it. Just try your best, mate, and remember, I'm always here for you.'

He never once judged me, and when I got into fights with the other officers, he'd run over to me with the rest of them, but not once did he ever take his truncheon out. He'd be knelt on the floor, by my side, whispering to me to calm down and to listen to just his voice. He talked me down from lots of potential riots.

After a few months of putting up with the madness of C Unit though, I'd had enough. One morning this psycho came at me and told me he was going to kill me and that he had a blade in his cell with my name on it. I wasn't having that. I'd just heard that morning that my Irene had married some geezer called Dave and I was already in a rage, so I stood up, grabbed a jam jar and started to slash the loony's face up. I saw red, and couldn't stop, so it was a relief really when the guards jumped me or I might have killed the poor bloke. I was charged with GBH, got a week in the box... and then put back on the unit.

I couldn't cope with the place, I couldn't cope knowing my Irene was now with another man, and I couldn't believe I was never going to see my son again. I tried to top myself in my cell, but unknown to me, I'd been put on suicide watch as they'd all noticed the change in me and, no sooner had I started trying to slit my wrists with a shard of glass, then the screws charged in. I wasn't ready for it, but I did manage to grab one of them and I beat the fuck out of him before they could stop me. I just thanked God it wasn't Mr Connell as I got dragged off. I knew I'd be shipped out again, but had no clue to where. Imagine my surprise when I was told I was subject to a transfer direct order under the Mental Health Act and I was being sent to Broadmoor Hospital for the criminally insane. I was gutted.

It was December 1978 when I arrived at Broadmoor and although I knew it was technically a hospital, I also knew it was a jail for the mad men.

I was surprised as I was taken through to booking that it actually did look more like a hospital rather than the grim, grey prisons I'd become accustomed to. This isn't too bad, I thought, as I watched staff walking by, dressed in white coats rather than prison officer garb. This could be a walk in the park for me. I hated that they'd certified me a mad man, of course, I guessed that title would stick for years but still, if I could do the rest of my sentence out in a place like this, it might be cushty. I'd already noticed the big gardens as I was escorted out of the transport, and the men tending to the flowers and plants. I liked a bit of gardening myself and I was now being told that there were lots of workshops here, a gymnasium, a music room and an area to watch TV. Fuck me, it sounded like a holiday camp, this place.

I soon realised, however, just how difficult this 'holiday camp' really was. I thought I'd seen some nutters on C Unit at Parkhurst, but these fuckers here were off the scale. Within weeks I witnessed men running into walls using their own heads as rams. You couldn't write it, they would do this over and over again until they fell unconscious. They would stab themselves with anything they could get their hands on, screaming out while they jabbed needles, pens, scissors into themselves. It was utter madness, and so many of them were subjected to forced medication, leaving them dribbling in a chair, unable to move or speak. One man stabbed himself in the eye with plastic scissors, rendering himself blind, but as soon as he came off the ward, complete with eye patch, he tried to rip off his own testicle, fucking madness.

Then there was this other geezer who used to try and eat himself. I couldn't believe it, but he actually bit chunks out of his own arms, legs and feet, it was disgusting. I had no clue how I'd get myself a transfer out, so I did the only thing I knew had always guaranteed it, I started beating people up. Doctors, guards, nutters, whoever I could get my hands on really. I needed out. This time I wasn't as discerning as I had been in the past because they were all as bad as each other!

It worked, but not as I expected. I mean, what was I thinking? I was one of 'them' now, the criminally insane. Why I thought I'd get back to a normal prison, I don't know.

I was shipped off to the maximum-security psychiatric jail, Rampton. My head was a mess as I tried desperately to work out how I could prove I wasn't insane. If I thought Broadmoor was a nightmare due to its inhabitants, it had nothing on Rampton. I was treated like an animal from the moment I got there, injected with all kinds of shite that had me just like the loonies I'd seen previously – dribbling, off my head, unable to walk straight or talk coherently, it was a fucking nightmare that I couldn't wake up from.

Somewhere deep inside my fuddled brain I managed to work out that I needed to stay quiet for a bit, keep my head down and allow the medication to leave my system without them feeling they needed to give me more. Only then would I be fit enough to do something that might get me out of there. So that's what I did. I spent two days silently sitting in an old armchair, watching the lunatics going about their business in the asylum.

Every time a doctor or nurse walked by, I'd close my eyes as though I was out of it or asleep, but my ears were wide open. I listened to everything that was said and, in doing this, I learned that the medicated geezer in the armchair opposite me was, in fact, a fucking beast. A nonce who'd raped young girls and murdered them, John White. I formulated a plan as I realised he might be my ticket out of Rampton.

When the opportunity presented itself, I was still a bit wobbly, and my head a bit fuzzy, but I was compos mentis enough to slowly pull the cord that was holding my dressing gown together, until I had it in my hands. I wrapped it around both wrists and then made a lunge for White, quickly wrapping the cord around his neck and pulling it tightly backwards. I wanted to strangle him, both for what he'd done, and to get me ghosted out. His eyes bulged out of their sockets as he tried in vain to get me off him. The other patients simply glanced over and went about their business, not one of them tried to stop me. I could hear a strange gurgling coming from White's throat as I pulled harder and I realised it was a death rattle. It was then I felt the needle going into my arm and I was aware that I was surrounded by white coats. I passed out and woke up in a padded cell. I was getting ghosted alright, straight back to fucking Broadmoor!

I was so depressed as I was once again being booked in and wondered if I was now on the same roundabout I'd been on with the normal jails, only this time I was destined to spend years being shunted backwards and forwards between the nut houses.

I suddenly remembered Irene's warning about where I was going to end up unless I learned to play the game with the system, and this made me even more depressed. Had she known, all those years ago, that I was in fact an actual nut case? I sincerely hoped not and although she'd started a new life without me in it now, just the thought of her was enough to make me stand up straighter and stop acting like a no hoper. This was in my thoughts as I was led through the hospital once again and there, grinning at me in the corridor, was my old friend, Ronnie Kray. I was over the moon and ran to hug him straight away. This man would raise my spirits, I knew it for sure!

Within a week, I realised that Ronnie was something of a celebrity in this place. He was treated with the utmost respect and he didn't seem to mind the lunatics one bit. In fact, I laughed when he told me he had a few of them on his pay roll. He actually did, too. Three muppets running around for him, making him cups of tea all day, taking him his newspaper, and even polishing his shoes. It was mad, but in a funny way.

CHAPTER TWENTY-ONE

IRENE

AS THE years went by, I had another baby with Dave. Baby James came along when my little girl was just three years old and Mike loved him as much as he loved his sister, Leicia. He was very protective of them both and would always watch over them.

'You go in the shop, Mum and I'll watch over the pram,' he would say if we went shopping. And he would guard the pram as if his life depended on it.

The relationship between Dave and Mike, however, was still fraught with difficulties, and I would often find myself standing outside a room, listening in, if the two of them were alone together. It was an awful feeling, but something I felt I had to do because I would always intervene if I thought Dave was picking on Mike. You know, I thought that it would make Mike resent his siblings, seeing how Dave clearly loved them and not him, but it didn't. My boy didn't have a bad bone in his body and it seemed to make him happy to watch Dave playing with the babies in a way he never had with him. I'd watch Mike, smiling at the happy family scene and it broke my heart really, but I was pleased it hadn't made him resentful.

Dave and I were growing apart too, I think, though I didn't realise it. I suffered from terrible coughs, I always had, and it was worse at night. Dave would toss and turn in bed, tutting and moaning, making me feel worse. So, in the end, I used to get up and go make up a bed on the settee downstairs so that we could both try to get some sleep. My dreams were still filled with thoughts about Mick because even though I had stopped writing a long time ago, the newspapers were still filled with worrying and often frightening stories about him. Hostage-taking, rooftop protests, harming other prisoners, it was endless and I was so torn between believing all I read, or listening to my inner voice that always stood up for Mick, reminding me of the man he always was to me. Then, of course, I'd feel guilty about it, because I was married to Dave and I shouldn't still be clinging to the past, but I couldn't help it. I'd often see Dave trying to make a real effort to please me and that would make me feel even more guilty.

'Me and my Dad are going to take Mike fishing with us,' he said one day when Mike was 11. 'It's about time we had a bit of male bonding, don't you think?'

I was surprised, but pleased to know that it was something Mike wanted too. 'I think that would be great,' I said. 'My Dad used to take him fishing when he was little, he'll love it.'

'I can only try, Irene,' he said. 'Let's see how it goes.'

That last sentence dampened any happiness I was feeling and made me feel nervous about the trip. I realised then that Dave wasn't really doing this for Mike, but to try to curry favour with me. The forced niceness didn't last though and Dave was soon back to always being on at Mike for one thing or another. It used to really upset me and I was living on my nerves for years, so goodness knows how Mike must have felt.

As the years went by, it became worse. As Mike grew older and the arguments became horrible to witness, I often thought it might come to a physical fight, but thank goodness it didn't. By the time Mike turned 16, things were really bad. One day they'd set to it because Mike hadn't done a job that Dave had instructed him to do and it quickly escalated to a completely different level.

'Get your stuff and leave!' Dave screamed in my son's face.

'Where am I meant to go, dickhead?' Mike yelled back.

'I don't care where you go, go to your grandparents, or your mate's house, anywhere, but you've had it here, lad, get gone and I don't want to see your face again, you hear?'

'That suits me,' Mike said and then ran upstairs to pack a bag.

Two minutes later he was gone. I was devastated and cried my eyes out for hours, believing I should have done more to intervene, but I was just so drained with the constant shouting and screaming between the two of them, I didn't have the strength left in me to fight it. A week later, just after Dave had set off to work, I was so happy because Mike sneaked up the drive and into the house to see me. I gave him a big hug and asked him how he'd been, but before we had the chance to catch up, Dave's car pulled back up on the drive. He'd obviously forgotten something. I was terrified and so was Mike, so he ran out to the garage to hide. Bloody Dave decided he'd stay home for another couple of hours for some reason and I was a nervous wreck thinking he might go out to the garage and discover Mike hidden there, it was awful. After Dave left, I was gutted to find that Mike had left. Poor lad must have got sick of waiting.

By now I'd started a new job and I was really enjoying it. I was working at a clothing retailer, Ethel Austin. It was a great place to shop for kids' clothes and underwear. I soon made friends with all the staff and some of the regular customers, one of whom was my Mum. She used to come in for her big knickers and support tights, as we were well-known in the area for having such a large and varied selection. The other shop assistants and me would often meet up for a drink after work at a pub called the Johnny Pye. It had a great atmosphere. One night I was in there, in my uniform, and this lady came up to me.

'I see you work at Ethel Austin,' she said, nodding at my uniform, 'and I hope you don't mind me saying, but I've noticed you quite a few times. You're the lady who travels to work on your bike, aren't you?'

It seemed a little weird, but I smiled at her. 'I am,' I said. 'I don't live that far away, and it keeps me fit, so…'

'Would you mind if I popped in tomorrow, while you're at work and took a photo of you?' she asked. 'I'm not a weirdo or anything, I just like to take photos of normal people, doing normal things, and then I paint them in oils. I'd love to paint you, your long black hair is always in plaits and it would look stunning in oil.'

'Oh, wow! I don't know what to say,' I said, laughing. 'But yes, I suppose, and what do you do with your paintings?'

'I display them and sell them,' she said. 'In fact, do you know the new cafe that's just opened on the high street?' she continued as I nodded. 'I'm doing a display of my work in there in two weeks, yours would be ready by then if you want to pop in and take a look.'

I was tickled by the idea and told her I'd be there. Two weeks later, me, my Mum and the kids went to the cafe to check out the lady's work. The first thing I saw as we walked in was this huge oil painting of me in all my glory. It really was an excellent likeness and as I scanned all the other paintings, I could tell the woman was brilliant at what she did. My Mum was thrilled at my portrait and she asked the woman if she could buy it to hang on her wall.

'You certainly can,' the lady said 'it's £300.'

'What?' My Mum asked, almost choking, 'I'm going to have to leave it then.'

It was such a shame it was so expensive and, like my Mum said as we were leaving, what the hell was she going to do with an unsold painting of me? It seemed silly to put such a high price tag on it. Still, the woman had been one of our more notable customers and she was a great artist. Another notable customer was a man we all called, 'the knicker feeler'. He would come in almost every day just to feel the knickers. Honestly, he was disgusting, he would walk straight to the back wall where we displayed all the skimpy thongs and he would systematically stroke the crotch of every single pair. It would have been too embarrassing for any of us to throw him out and, besides, after each visit he would buy a skimpy thong to take home. We all knew they weren't for his wife, we'd seen her and she was a big lady, no way would she have fit into those thongs.

The best day ever at Ethel Austin was my 50th birthday. All my friends blindfolded me before letting me into the store, and when I went in, they tore my blindfold off and all the staff shouted, 'surprise!' They'd done a huge party for me with food, balloons and presents and my main gift

– which they'd all put money in to buy – was a brand new bicycle. I couldn't believe it and burst into tears. They'd all noticed for ages how I'd been struggling with my old bike as the chain kept slipping off and they'd gone and bought me a beautiful new one. It was so thoughtful, they were just like my second family.

My first family, however, was not so jolly right now. Dave and I argued most days, and it made me feel bitter that I felt I'd sacrificed some of Mike's happiness in order to keep things on an even keel in my marriage. I also felt guilty that Mike only had me, his brother and sister, and my parents, and that was my fault too. I deeply regretted stopping contact with Mick's family because I know for a fact that they'd have been a great support to him as he was growing up. I'd prevented any of that and Mike hadn't asked for it. He was too young to understand at the time and would have simply accepted it. But now, as a young man, he must be questioning it, and I felt terrible for him and for Joe and Eira, because they had loved him dearly.

I mentioned it to my Mum one day when I took the little ones round. She made a pot of tea and told me to sit down.

'Irene, I wondered when you might feel like this, love,' she said. 'There's something you should know.'

My heart leapt and I had an awful feeling in my stomach. I assumed she was going to tell me that one of Mick's family had died or something.

'What Mum? What's happened?'

'Nothing bad, love, or at least I hope you won't think it's bad, but ever since Mike was a little boy, I've kept in touch with Joe and Eira. I phoned them regularly to keep them updated on Mike. They begged me to, I'm so sorry, Irene. I thought I was doing the right thing.'

I stood up and hugged my Mum, relief and happiness washing over me, 'Oh, Mum, you did. You did do the right thing and I'm so happy you did, I've been feeling ever so guilty.'

'Oh, thank god, Irene,' Mum said, almost crying. 'I was so afraid you'd go mad. I've sent them photos too, every year so they could see how big and handsome he was getting. Was that alright too?'

'Yes, yes, Mum, I'm so happy you did all that, and I know they must hate me for what I did, I just didn't know what else to do.'

'They don't hate you at all, love,' Mum said. 'They did understand after you remarried. They were disappointed, how could they not be? But they understood and they respected your decision. They even told me that Mick understood it too.'

My life seemed to be filled with a series of coincidences, and this news from my Mum, which filled me with happiness for some reason, was followed by yet another surprising revelation the very next day.

I'd gone in to work as usual when Sandra, one of the

other assistants, whistled at me from the office door. She put her hand up to her ear and mouthed 'phone call' to me, so I finished up with my customer and ran to the office. I always dreaded a phone call at work, always assuming it would be something bad or sad, so I was surprised that it was my auntie calling.

'Bit of a strange one this, Irene,' she said, 'only, I got a phone call last night from a man who asked if I was any relation to you and, if so, could I give him your phone number.'

'What?' I asked, puzzled and also a bit worried. 'Who was it? Did he say? You didn't give him my number, did you?'

'Of course I didn't,' auntie replied. 'I'm not daft. All he said was that he was an old friend of Mick's and he needed to get in touch with you about something. I didn't ask what, but I did get his number and told him I'd pass the message on to you, so that's what I'm doing.'

'Oh dear,' I said. 'I wonder who it is and what he wants.' Auntie laughed.

'Irene, you know how you'll get the answers, don't you? Bloody phone him!'

So that's exactly what I did, after pacing the floor when I got home from work, then having a bath and thinking about it some more. In the end, the suspense was killing me, so I picked up the phone and rang the man.

'Hello, Ray Williams here,' the voice at the end of the phone said. 'Can I help you?'

'Um, it's Irene, Mick's ex-wife,' I said, suddenly feeling silly. This man could be an axe murderer for all I knew. What the hell was I doing?

'Ah, Irene,' he said. 'I was hoping you'd get in touch. Like I said to your Aunt, I believe, I'm a good friend of Mick's. I have been for years, and I stayed in touch with him while he's been in… well, you know. Anyhow, and I hope you don't mind me being the messenger, but Mick's been trying to trace you for a few years without any luck.'

'Me? What for? Has something happened?' Right away my mind leapt straight away to thinking the worst.

'No, no,' Ray said, 'nothing's wrong, Irene, I promise, it's just, he'd like to reach out to his boy even if you don't want to hear from him. I know it's been a long time, but…'

'Too right it's been a long time,' I said. 'It's been 26 bloody years to be accurate, so why now?' I was shaking suddenly and had to sit down and hold on to the sideboard as I felt faint.

'I can imagine how you must be feeling,' Ray said, 'and like I said, I apologise for being the bearer of all this. I know though, that Mick has tried many times to try to find you both over the years, but, well, there's only so much you can do from behind bars, I guess. The thing is, Mick has never forgotten either you or Mike. There hasn't been a day when he's not thought or spoke about you and, well, he'd really, really love to try to reconnect with your Mike if he's up for it.'

My head was spinning, suddenly all those newspaper headlines I'd seen over the years came flooding back to me, like actual newspapers smacking me in the face. All the horrible stories I'd seen and heard on the news and from gossips. I felt afraid and alone and I didn't know what to say.

'Look, Irene, I know this must be a shock,' Ray said after what seemed like an eternity. 'I tell you what. Why don't I let you get off the phone now so you can have a think about things and maybe talk to your Mike about it. Then, if you or he decide you want to get in touch with Mick, just phone me back – no rush. I'll sort everything out for you. Does that sound fair?'

'Thank you, I appreciate that,' I said, relieved he wasn't expecting an answer there and then. 'And I will think about it, I promise. Either way I will get back to you and let you know what I decide to do. I won't just leave you wondering, Ray, and thanks for doing this for Mick, I'm sure he will appreciate it whatever the outcome.'

My mind was in complete turmoil and there was only one person I felt safe speaking to about it, and that was my Mum.

'What a turn up,' she said after I explained everything. 'After all these years. Have you told Mike? What did he say?'

'No, Mum, I haven't told Mike,' I said. 'That's why I'm here, to ask you what I should do!'

Mum tutted and put the kettle on.

'Well, I'm sure I can't tell you what to do, Irene, that's completely up to you. Besides, when have you ever listened to me? Particularly when it concerned Mick.'

'Oh, mother!' I said. 'Of course I listen to you, and I know it's down to me to decide in the end, but I'm asking, what would you do if you were me?'

Mum sighed, poured the tea and then sat at the table with me.

'He deserves to know, I think,' she said. 'No matter what's happened in the past, no matter what Mick has or hasn't done, he's the boy's father, Irene. And I hate to point this out, but look how guilty you've been feeling recently about the contact between the boy and his other grandma and grandad.'

'I'm scared of his reaction though, Mum,' I said. 'What if he flips his lid and goes mad at me for even suggesting it.'

'Has he ever said anything to suggest that might happen if you talk about his Dad?' Mum asked.

I shook my head.

'Mum, I've never mentioned him. I act like Mick didn't exist, and I hate that I've done that, Mum, I hate it.' I started to cry then, and Mum rushed to hug me.

'Irene, lovey, don't get upset. What's done is done, and there's no use crying over spilt milk, babbi. Take my advice and tell Mike all about the call. Apologise to him for never talking about his Dad if that will make you feel better, but my inkling is that he won't hold any of that against you and he'll be curious to know more about his real Dad.'

In the end, Mum was right. Of course she was, mums are always right – most of the time, anyway. Mike was shocked at first, and I watched the colour drain out of his face as he took in what I was saying.

'If I went to see him, would you be coming with me, Mum?' he asked.

'No, son,' I said. 'I don't think that would be a good idea, but from what I understand, the guy who I spoke to, Ray, would go with you if you wanted him to. I mean, you'd have to meet up with him beforehand, so you could get to know him a bit first, but yeah, he'd go with you.'

It was as if I'd suddenly unlocked a secret diary for Mike. He had loads of questions for me, but not once did he blame me for cutting ties with his Dad and his family. In fact, he made it clear that he understood I'd done it for his benefit. He'd managed to get through school without anybody giving him grief about his Dad and where he was, and that was mainly because we'd kept all that information from him. Mike decided to get in touch with Ray the next day and they arranged to meet.

Three weeks later, they were travelling to have Mike's visit with Mick.

CHAPTER TWENTY-TWO

MICK

I STARTED to go through a period of depression, I think, the second time I was in Broadmoor. I was angry that, according to the newspapers, according to prison sources, and according to the doctors, I was simply a violent thug. Broadmoor couldn't decide if I was a psychopath or a schizophrenic but, either way, they decided I had no regard for the rules or for others. I was actually a fucking mass of rage and hurt and these bastards had contributed to that. I knew I was in grave danger of losing my head completely.

Ronnie Kray helped me a lot and tried to keep me calm and happy and I appreciated it. One day he came to me when I was feeling particularly low and said he had a surprise for me.

'You know with my connections and the like,' Ronnie said, making me laugh as he put on a high and mighty act for me. 'Well, through those connections, I've managed to sort you out a very special visit, my boy. You can thank me later.'

'Go on then,' I said. 'Who you got coming in for me, not one of them filthy women again, Ronnie, only the last one almost snapped in half when I hugged her.' I joked back.

'Think dashing, think bashing, think Paddington Express,' Ronnie said.

I stared at him in disbelief.

'You're fucking kidding,' I said. 'You mean Terry Downes? Why would he come see me, Ron?'

'The very man,' Ronnie said. 'One of the best boxers of all time if you ask me, and as for why, well, it's because I requested it, Micky. I wanted to cheer you up a bit.'

Ronnie did that for me and I was so grateful. Terry Downes was a World Champion, I was in awe of him. I had watched him fight many times and it was obvious how he'd earned his nickname, the Paddington Express, because it must have felt like being hit by a train if he clipped you. He was such an aggressive boxer, but I recognised his style because I felt I shared that kind of fast determination to win and end a fight. Prolonging the pain was never something on my radar when fighting, all my senses simply went into this hyper-alert mode, and I could see what needed to be done to end it in my favour. I always liked to think that Downes had that mentality. We had a very enjoyable visit, he told me about how he'd recently been in training to act in a movie and we talked about our parents and boxing in general, it was great, and I did thank Ronnie afterwards.

A day like that would see me happy for a while, maybe a few weeks even, but in a place like Broadmoor, it could never last for long. In my opinion, the staff, doctors, nurses and officers should have been trained to look out for warning signs, but they didn't give a fuck. When you are touched by madness, every single minute of every single day, what did they think was going to happen? Now, it might be just me, but I don't think it takes a fucking psychology degree to work it out.

There was this big mouthy bastard, Gordon Robinson was his name, and he did everybody's nut in, always shouting his mouth off at someone, always getting in my fucking way. I couldn't stand him and, one day, when I was feeling really down, something just snapped and Robinson just happened to be the first person I saw when I flipped. I grabbed hold of a tie off someone and ran to him and wrapped the tie around his neck. I didn't have any thoughts of killing him, I just needed him to shut the fuck up, but I couldn't stop strangling him, I just couldn't. It wasn't like the last time I'd done it, where I could look at the geezer's face, I couldn't see anything, it was like my rage was a cloudy smoke, obstructing my vision. Suddenly I staggered backwards and I was shocked out of my blind rage as I watched Robinson slump to the floor. I looked at my hands and noticed the silk tie I'd been using had snapped. That was the moment I was stabbed with a needle and dragged off to segregation.

I was fucking livid when I came round. Outraged they'd done that to me again, and not only to subdue me from that incident, they then kept me subdued for days after. That's not for any other reason than to teach a person a lesson and I'm not stupid, that is not what a hospital should be about. Lunatic asylum or not. When I was sent back to the main hospital, I started asking questions of those who were lucid and not brain dead. I wanted to know why they didn't stand up for themselves and demand better treatment. Given my reputation I had no doubt I wouldn't be there for long, but some of these poor fuckers had been here years and would probably never get out. Why did they accept all this shit?

'You'll never beat 'em, Micky,' Ronnie said, when I told him that nobody had the guts to speak out for fear of forced medication as a punishment. 'You can't keep on fighting for everybody, just yourself, mate, or you'll end up doing fucking life.'

'I don't care, Ronnie,' I said. 'It's a fucking liberty, mate. Not enough that we're stuck in this place, they have to try to tame the fight out of you as well. It's a fucking hospital, Ron, they're meant to help us get better, not stick us with fucking needles just 'cos we won't bow down to them.'

I formulated a plan, and a week later I had made my

way on to the roof of Broadmoor. Fuck me, all hell broke loose when they knew about it. I was a very strong man, very strong, so the slate tiles were no trouble to me at all, and I wasted no time ripping them off and piling them up. The tiles were now my weapons, and as soon as all the guards were out and shouting up to me, I started pelting them down like missiles. Hit a few of them too. Life for the other prisoners had to carry on as normal of course, and I could have kicked myself when I saw Violet Kray being escorted through the crowd that had gathered. I immediately stopped throwing the tiles and shouted down to her.

'Hello, Mrs Kray' I said, smiling. 'Please tell Ronnie I never knew you were visiting today and give him my best.'

'I will do, Micky,' she shouted back. 'You be careful up there, son, don't you fall.'

The minute she was inside, I started my rampage again and pretty soon I noticed the TV cameras and press vans arriving. I waved at all of them and screamed out my protest at the treatment we were getting, then I continued trying to hit as many of the staff as I could with my tiles.

Years of being in the block and being almost starved in the strongboxes must have prepared my body to be able to take all kinds of punishment, because I was on that rooftop for three days without food, water or sleep. I was finally talked down by one of the bosses, who'd brought my Mum and Dad over to help him and who promised me the world on a fucking plate. I knew it was bullshit, they were just sick of all the publicity I was causing and all the questions they were being asked. But I came down because I wanted to, not because they wanted me to. I'd done what I set out to do and that was to let the world know about the barbaric conditions in this hospital, and to demand more humane treatment for the patients. Did it work? Fuck knows really, but I do know that I wasn't injected with anything this time when they threw me into segregation.

'Time to reflect, Peterson,' is what they said.

'Time for some fucking shut eye,' I replied with a wink as I settled down on my rock hard bed.

A few months later I staged another protest from the roof and was told I caused £250,000 worth of damage. I had no idea, but if you ask me, they deserved it. In Broadmoor you are less than an animal and no one cares.

'I think it's alright, Micky,' Ronnie told me. 'In fact, I was happy to be transferred here. At least you can do stuff to keep you busy, a bit of gardening or farm work if you wanna get your hands dirty. You get to walk around, have free visits, read a paper in peace. Shit, I even have my own fucking barber!'

I laughed at that, because it was true. Ronnie had a fellow come in to do his hair, tailor his fucking suits and the other inmates bent over backwards to do stuff for him, like make his tea in his favourite china cup, or clean his room. He'd learned to accept the system and manipulate it to his benefit.

'You have to play the game a bit, Micky, start seeing the shrink like I do. You tell 'em what you're feeling, talk about whatever shit you want once you're in their office, the worse you make it, the better it is for you in the long run. The way I look at it is, it's like when we were on the outside, playing the long game with a punter, knowing that in the end we'd get what we wanted. You start telling that shrink all about your treatment in here and elsewhere and I guarantee he makes things happen for you.'

A lot of people wrote Ronnie Kray off, said he was a mad man, but I know he was a very intelligent man in reality. He was troubled, of course, weren't we all in a way? But he always knew what he wanted and how to get it.

I followed his advice and booked an appointment with the shrink. Ronnie was right, soon after I was presented with books, paper, pens and pencils and given free access to the art studio. I started writing poems and stories and trying out drawings and paintings. It really helped to pass the time and keep me calm and for a long time things were easier for me. As the months flew by though, I started to get itchy feet again, and some new inmates were starting to get right on my nerves. I ended up hitting one of them one day, but instead of waiting for my reprimand, I was back up on the roof. This time I was demanding a transfer, I was sick of it.

They talked me down again within the day, promising to look at transferring me and, like an idiot, I believed them. It was only when I was back in segregation that they told me through the hatch that it wasn't happening. I was fuming that I'd given in so easily, so I decided I'd go on a hunger strike. I refused to eat anything until they agreed to listen to me.

The strike lasted 18 days and it made me really ill, but it worked. Suddenly, they decided to declare that I was no longer certified mad. Really? Because they wanted rid of me, I was no longer a mad man? Stupid, but great for me. In June 1984 I was granted a transfer to Park Lane Hospital. Still a nut house I understood, but not Broadmoor, so I hoped it might be better conditions.

CHAPTER TWENTY-THREE

IRENE

OVER THE next few years, I kept on seeing Mick on television for various rooftop protests and it seemed that he'd also started to take hostages to make demands for better treatment in prison. I could watch things like this now without guilt or fear. Dave and I had divorced. I was no longer having scary dreams about Mick and I was captivated when I saw him on screen or in a paper because he was always the showman. It would make me giggle sometimes when I'd heard he'd said something funny or very inappropriate because I knew he was only doing it for a reaction. Like one time he'd apparently taken someone hostage and then demanded tea, biscuits and a blow-up doll. Of course, he didn't really want those things, he'd said it to wind the screws up and he knew it would make the news, they must have known that.

One day I got a phone call from someone at Channel 4,

saying they were making a documentary about Mick and would I be a part of it. Next, Channel Five phoned to ask me the same thing. They were both making documentaries, I couldn't believe it. Both were offering me large sums of money to appear and they were competing with each other to get me to be only on their show. I agreed to go on one, but not the other. The one I had not agreed to came out first, and it really, truly shocked and upset me. Despite me telling them I refused to cooperate, they used my images, photos of me with Mick, and used quotes I definitely did not say. I was fuming, but what upset me the most was the violent and horrible treatment that Mick had been getting. Someone had sneaked video footage out of the prison and sold it to the documentary makers and now it was being aired on national television.

'Mum, Mum!' Leicia called to me the day it was aired. 'Come look, Mum, you have to see this. You're on the telly!'

She was right, there was a photo of me on the screen and a commentator in the background quoting things I was meant to have said. I was furious! But that subsided into sadness as I watched the leaked video footage. I was transfixed, tears ran down my cheeks as I watched Mick being taunted and beaten by a mob of around 15 screws. The documentary also went into some of the terrible conditions in the particular jail that Mick was currently in and spoke about all the horrors he'd endured over the years. It was very, very upsetting, I couldn't bear it and I couldn't sleep that night for worrying about him.

The next day I went out shopping to our local Tesco and I was so surprised to find that complete strangers were coming up to me to speak.

'Your poor husband,' one woman said. 'I was shocked when I watched that last night. You stay strong, my love.'

'It's certainly changed my mind,' another woman said as she gave me a hug. 'Those bastards who done that to him want stringing up for it, they really do.'

I hadn't watched it through to the end myself, as it upset me too much, so I was doubly shocked when a third woman ran down the aisle after me.

'I couldn't believe it when they blamed you, Irene, love, how the hell was it your fault? You haven't been married to Mick for years.'

'Blamed me for what?' I asked. 'I couldn't bring myself to watch it all.'

'Oh, they said because you divorced him, he lost his marbles, said it was your fault he became Bronson and went mad. Bloody cheek if you ask me, Irene, and I tell you what, I used to call him a nutcase myself, but never again, not after I've seen what he's gone through, poor bugger.'

I couldn't believe they'd done that on television. All I'd ever done was love Mick, and he must have known that. I knew there was no way he would have implied any of what happened afterwards was my fault. I vowed to be really careful when I was filmed for my documentary, to make sure I didn't say anything that could be taken out of context. I started to make lots of notes to help me on the day, so I wouldn't forget anything that I wanted to say. I had bought myself a beautiful new dress to wear for the filming and some matching clip-on earrings, all from a little boutique I liked, and then I felt prepared for anything.

The documentary was going to include footage from lots of different people, including Mick's family, but we were all being filmed at different times. Thankfully mine and Mike's parts were being done on the same day, so, armed with all my notes, we met the crew in a local pub for a drink to calm our nerves. Leicia was there with us, too, she found it all really exciting and we were really put at ease. The crew were so lovely and we had a good laugh with them all.

I was then taken to the area that would be the backdrop to my interview. It was in Ellesmere Port, down by the river Mersey. A place I'd known so well but hardly recognised it now as it had all been built up with posh apartments and landscaped areas. The Mersey was glistening in the sunshine too, giving me a lovely background. My nerves were soon calmed when I realised that these filmmakers were happy to portray only the truth and they allowed me to keep on stopping the filming so I could check on my notes. They let me say exactly what I wanted to say and afterwards they smiled at me and said it was one of the nicest interviews they'd ever done.

Mike's interview was done in a hilly, grassy area, which was also lovely, and every now and again, a train went by in the distance. We had such a laugh though, because suddenly this man appeared out of nowhere and stripped all of his clothes off – doing a streak, then ran right in front of the cameras. It was hilarious and we all had to stop filming until we could stop laughing and start again. Neither Mike nor myself felt under any pressure whatsoever and we both felt very comfortable about what we'd shared that day. This documentary, when it aired, was honest and real, and certainly didn't glamourise any violence.

A few days later, I was back at work, dressed in my usual Ethel Austin uniform, hair in plaits, working on the tills. The till area was positioned right by the front door, so anyone coming in would have to walk right by me. I enjoyed working this area because it meant I got to say hi to all my regulars when they came in. I was chatting away to a customer after she'd paid for her new dress when the staff buzzer went off. It was like a walkie talkie type of thing that stayed by the till and was only used if the manager needed us for something. I picked it up and pressed the button to hear.

'Irene, take off your name badge and come up to the office straight away, love, don't speak to anybody.'

Bloody hell, I thought, what on earth have I done now, and why do I need to take off my name badge? I did as she asked and rushed up to her office.

'The press are here, Irene,' she said. 'They're asking for you. I wouldn't confirm that you worked here, but they've gone back down to the shop floor. I don't know what they want, but I'm guessing it's something to do with that documentary. You should put your coat on to cover your pinafore and sneak out the back. I'll see you tomorrow.'

'Oh my God,' I said, 'they must have walked right by me downstairs. Jesus! I hope I'm not followed.'

'Back door, love.' the manager said. 'Go grab your coat and I'll go back down to the shop and make sure no one spots you.'

I couldn't believe it and rushed home on my bike as fast as I could, only to get home and find a letter addressed to me from the *Daily Mirror*. It seemed they were doing an article about Mick and wanted to pay me a large sum of money to spill the beans on what life had really been like living with him. Someone from the paper then phoned me to follow up and suggested that it was better if I cooperated with them rather than any other paper who might be in touch. I declined. There was no way I was going to accept anything that would no doubt upset somebody somewhere. Mick's family deserved some peace now, I thought.

Another nice thing that came out of the documentary I

did was I went back to the little boutique where I'd bought my dress and earrings, as I wanted to buy a handbag I'd noticed. The lady who served me remembered me.

'Oh, I meant to thank you, Irene, next time you came in. I've sold three more of those dresses you bought that day. Different women who saw you on the TV loved your look and came in to buy it for themselves, so thank you, and ten per cent off your handbag!'

Lots of stories came out about Mick and about Mike and me over the next year or two. Some good, some bad, but the worst part was that we had no control over any of them. One story, which I can't go into as it wasn't mine, affected my son really, really, badly. So much so, that he needed help to get over it, and it devastated me that one of my children should hurt so much. I've always prided myself on being a strong woman, but seeing Mike go through what he did, I was like a wounded animal and wanted to lash out at the world. The urge to simply scream was overwhelming and for days I would hide out in my bedroom and just roar and scream until I couldn't anymore. I was like somebody possessed, I'd swear at the top of my voice and howl. It was awful, and though my family didn't say anything, I noticed that whenever I went anywhere during that time, there was always one of them there to accompany me.

A few years later, when Mick was, of course, still in prison, I received some legal documents to sign about a film they wanted to make about him. They wanted my permission for someone to portray me. But on reading the contract and getting my brother-in-law to read it and explain to me what it entailed – it was all in legal jargon and I didn't have a clue what it all meant – I decided not to sign it and never sent the contract back to them. There was a rumour at the time that Michael Winner wanted to produce the film, although I didn't hear anything about that afterwards.

A long time after that, I was told that Tom Hardy was going to play Mick in the film. I wasn't consulted about anything in this movie, even though they had an actress playing me in it. When it was released, and about to be shown in cinemas around the country, a couple of the girls from work went upstairs at the cinema in Liverpool One to look at the advertising posters of coming films. When they came back, they told me that Mick's film, Bronson, was advertised and that there was a big poster of Mick and, on his arm, they said he had a heart tattoo with an arrow through it saying Irene. Ah, I was touched, even though I didn't know when or how Mick could have had that tattoo done, because when we were together Mick didn't have any tattoos.

I didn't go to the cinema to see the movie, I felt too emotional, but when it came out on DVD an ex-boyfriend played it on the TV as a surprise for me. It did upset me, and I couldn't bring myself to watch the whole thing. All the violence against Mick by the heavy mob was so upsetting for me, so I've never actually watched it to the end.

Now, Tom Hardy is a fabulous actor, and he performed the script he was given really well but, to be honest, the film did nothing at all for Mick. It portrayed him as some kind of maniac clown, and there was so much fabrication, and not enough of the real man portrayed in it. But that's the movies, I guess, they have to make it exciting so that everyone wants to see it. Also, they seemed to have got a lot of the part of myself and a girl who went to visit him in prison mixed up.

During this time, Mike and I also found out what was really happening to Mick in prison. It was so upsetting and worrying for us both. The horror of it all just went on and on and on and still to this day it's going on. I wanted Mick out of prison so much, especially for Mike. He had always really missed his Dad and needed him in his life – not in prison. Even though I had remarried and Mike was getting older, the effects were still really hitting us. We were at a loss, because, really, what can you do? Nothing, nothing at all. It's all out of your hands and because Mick had become 'Bronson', it was just getting harder and harder for us both to come to terms with it. A living nightmare which I wouldn't wish on anyone. The boy had visited his dad now, many times – but a prison visit wasn't enough to get to know somebody properly, was it?

CHAPTER TWENTY-FOUR

MICK

THINGS STARTED out okay at Park Lane, or Ashworth Hospital, as it became known. Unlike Broadmoor it was really modern and it seemed more organised. The facilities were good too, and the staff didn't seem as strict as they were at the last place, so I settled in for a bit as I became accustomed to my surroundings.

There were absolutely loads of shrinks here, more than at Broadmoor. Psychologists, psychiatrists, clinical this and clinical that, and I found myself bombarded with one doctor or another. It got on my nerves, answering the same questions over and over again, and talking about the same shit all the time. It didn't do me any good and it made me laugh that a system that had created me, was now trying to undo the damage, yet never taking any responsibility that I was the way I was because of them.

After a while, I couldn't take any more crap, and the

usual rage that was always bubbling away just below the surface erupted one day when another inmate, a bloke called Mervin Horley, made sexual advances towards me. I wasn't having that, and before I knew it, I'd grabbed a sauce bottle from the canteen table, smashed it and stabbed the fucker with it. You guessed it, that was the end of Ashworth. I pleaded guilty to GBH and got another three years added to my sentence.

Listen, it's safe to say that I would never settle in one place, and the prisons didn't want me making myself comfortable with them. They'd argue about who would take me and some even built special cells to hold me in. From Ashworth, I moved to general population back in Grisly Risley, but they soon dragged me off to segregation after punching someone up – cue another move, this time back to Walton, yay! My old stomping ground, but did I settle? Did I fuck, in fact I staged another rooftop protest to complain about the miserable conditions there. £100,000 worth of damage later, I had another year added.

I won't name all of the prisons that followed, but in 1986 I was transferred eight times! Fuck me, some stays were shorter than a fucking mini break at Bognor Regis. The only offence during all that time – well, the only offence I considered to be a bit naughty – was when I strangled the governor of Wormwood Scrubs. He never liked me anyway. In January 1987 I was transferred to a Cat B prison, HMP Gartree in Leicestershire, where

I spent the remainder of my never-ending sentence in isolation. Banged up, alone, for 23 hours a day. Great idea for someone about to be set free, don't you think?

Now here comes the interesting bit, I got set free. It was October 1987. A once normal, loving, family-oriented man, had been incarcerated for a crime that carried a tariff of seven years, but instead had spent 13 years behind the bars of some of the toughest, maximum-security jails in the country. I'd been tortured, beaten, starved, subjected to forced mind-altering drugs, and spent years in the most terrible segregated punishment blocks, isolated from any form of human contact. Had I deserved the extra years? Absolutely I did. But, did I deserve everything else I'd been subjected to? Absolutely not.

Throughout all of that, I had held firmly onto my sanity. I had seen men come back from just a few days in the block, changed forever, but I hadn't allowed myself to fall into that hole. The thing is, it took a kind of superhuman strength, and everything I had, just to keep my mind and body occupied and well. I had no room to concentrate on the normalities of life. Most men I knew, including Ronnie and Reggie, made their cells into homes. They pinned up photos and pictures, had new bedding and such brought in to make them more comfortable, but I could never do that. I could never think of a prison cell as my home, and I never treated it as such, so nothing adorned my walls, no home comforts were ever brought in because I wouldn't allow it. A prison is hell on earth and my cell was simply an extension of that.

My parents didn't know this new version of me, and I didn't know how to pull up any remnants of who I used to be to put them at ease. So, although I was pleased to see them when they came to pick me up, and I was grateful to have their home to stay in, I knew it couldn't last.

Ronnie and Reggie Kray had given me some really valuable connections in the fighting world and I had the number written down of a friend of theirs, fight promoter, Paul Edmonds, and I was assured that if I met up with him, he would set me up with some fights from which I'd make a lot of money. Trouble was, he was based in Luton, my hometown from being a kid. I stayed a couple of weeks with my Mum and Dad, just to get adjusted to how the world was right now and I found it really difficult. Cars, fashion, TV shows, everything was different, and even though by now I was an expert in adapting to the environment, I still felt like a fish out of water.

I caught a train to London, bought a toy gun, a water pistol to be exact, and used it to threaten a bloke to give me a lift to Luton. I can't believe he fell for it to be honest, but then again, I suppose I did look intimidating.

Paul Edmonds, as Ronnie and Reggie promised, was happy to see me, and after I'd introduced myself he immediately took me into his office for a chat and a drink..

'I've heard a lot about you, Mick,' he said. 'The twins say you're the toughest geezer they've ever met, and that's high praise indeed coming from them.

'They said you could hook me up with a few fights to make some good money,' I said. 'Legitimate matches and all.'

Paul laughed and slapped me on the back, a gesture I knew to be friendly.

'I don't know if my fights are considered strictly legit, Micky,' he said. 'They'll be unlicensed, but we can work on that, try to get it all sorted for you. In the meantime, the conditions will be just the same, proper ring, proper venues, big crowds, I guarantee you'll make money, mate, you up for that?'

I thought for a second and then nodded. I could do a few unlicensed fights until he got all my paperwork sorted, so I could go pro. I really wanted my Dad to see me do well. I wanted to make him proud, because I knew how much he loved and respected boxing.

'When do I start? I asked, grinning from ear to ear.

'Soon as,' Paul said. 'But first, we need to do something about changing your name.'

'What's wrong with my name?' I asked, feeling a bit of anger rising up. I was proud of my name.

'Nothing, Micky,' Paul said, quickly. 'Nothing at all, mate, I'm just thinking about it for your benefit. Think about it, Micky Peterson is an ex-con. No disrespect, mate, but with a new name, a real tough boxing name, it's like a fresh start, see?'

I did see, and I began to get excited then, thinking up new names. In the end, I settled on Charles Bronson after the tough guy movie star I'd heard good things about. Paul loved it, but I wasn't so sure. I'd have preferred Clint Eastwood, but he was having none of that, and within days my first unlicensed fight had been organised. It was to be at a big, posh venue too, the Bow Royal Theatre in London.

Now, an unlicensed fight doesn't exactly follow the Queensbury rules, so to speak, and although technically, bare knuckle and unlicensed fights are not breaking any laws, it still leaves the men involved open to prosecution if they were to really harm an opponent. The uninjured party couldn't claim taking part in a sport as a defence and my first fight was to be no different.

Round one started and the crowd were going wild, mainly for the guy I was up against, after all, I was an unknown. That all went okay and I knew I'd beat this mug. I landed every punch I threw. But in round two, it all went tits up. The bloke nutted me, and I went berserk. I knocked him to the floor and got on top of him, punching fuck out of his face. People were going mad, jumping in the ring, trying to pull me off. A lot of them were sticking the boot in too and punching me in the head. I eventually managed to stand up, but I staggered back slightly, and that was when my gun slipped out of my shorts and onto the canvas. That's right, I'd bought a gun, I'd bought a couple in fact.

The commentator saw the gun and decided to fucking announce it to all and sundry, and all hell broke loose. I was being attacked from all angles by a booing, angry mob. Paul tried to take charge of the situation and calm the crowd by disqualifying me and declaring the fight to the other geezer, and I was shunted off to the dressing room. It all seemed to cool off and Paul was urging me to hurry up and get changed, but suddenly, the dressing room door burst open and it all kicked off again, about ten of them screaming at me 'cos they'd lost money. That's when I remembered my second gun. I grinned, reached into my Lonsdale gym bag and pulled out a sawn-off shotgun. I waved it in the air, grinning like a nut case.

'If you lot don't fuck off,' I yelled. 'I'm gonna start shooting, one! Two!'

They fucked off before I got to number three and I was ushered outside and into Paul's car.

'You do realise the twins, Ronnie and Reggie, had five hundred quid on you to win that fight?' Paul said, clearly frustrated at the turn of events. 'Fuck me, Charlie, you'll be the death of me.'

He'd started to call me Charlie all the time now and I was getting used to it, in fact, I thought it suited me.

'Well, you said you had six fights lined up,' I said.

'There's not a man who can beat me, Paul, I promise you, tell the twins it'll be all good from now on. Five hundred quid is a lot of money, but they got plenty.'

I had the time of my life fighting. The twins must have been happy as Larry because I made them thousands over my next five matches. Proper money for them and I was on a good earn too. I was fucking gutted though when Paul gave me the news that the British Board of control of Boxing had refused me my boxing licence and said I'd never be able to go professional. It really hurt me, more than anything ever had really as I was counting on that for everything. I wanted to go legit. I had been born to fight and I know I had it in me to become a champion in the sport. I looked at the rejection paperwork and saw it had been declined because I'd been declared mad and was a previous patient of Broadmoor Hospital. My Dad had always told me, 'always get the first hit in, lad,' and that had always been my mantra during a fight. Not this time though, this time the system had got the first shot in, and even though I was out of it, they were still beating me.

I was depressed once again, my hopes and dreams crushed, and I didn't have the compass that other men at the age of 37 do. I was adrift, trying to appear normal, like everybody else, but I wasn't, was I? All these years, while other men had been bringing up families and going out to work, meeting mates who were role models, I'd been cast into a world of despair and isolation. I knew I only had myself to blame for going to prison in the first place, but I'd missed out on so many of life's lessons and I didn't know what to do about it.

Actually, I thought I did know what to do about it, but I was wrong. What I thought I needed was a good woman. Irene had long since made a new life for herself, so now I decided that's what I'd do. I would propose to my new, on-and-off girlfriend, and then maybe my life would start to take shape.

However, I needed a ring, but when I looked in the jeweller's shop windows, I was shocked to see the price of a decent one. Fuck it, I thought, I'll do just one more robbery, get the ring, then I'm done, that's all I need.

So, on New Year's Day, I went armed with a shotgun. The ring I fancied, a lovely diamond, was handed to me by a terrified jeweller and I ran off to propose to my girl-friend, Alison. Not only was I shocked to have her reject me, but to top it all, I was arrested for the job within days.

The arresting officers charged me under my new name, and it was at that point I decided I'd stick to Charles Bronson from now on and say goodbye to Micky Peterson.

Bedford Prison refused to take me on remand because of my behaviour the last time around, so I was sent to Leicester to await my trial. Another shithole of a prison. To be fair, my defence looked really good and I was told I could well get off of this because the witnesses had refused to testify for fear of reprisal. Alison was to be my alibi, she would say I was with her the whole time, so it all looked good.

Then a week before trial, by now I'd been moved again to Brixton, in June 1988, it all fell apart. Alison retracted her original statement and the cow went across to the prosecution as a main witness, which is all they needed to get me. My solicitor told me my only hope was to cooperate and plead guilty, which I did. I pleaded guilty to armed robbery and was given seven years. I was placed in a special unit of 16 prisoners in Brixton. Top security, yet again!

Of course, it didn't stop there, Wandsworth, Full Sutton, Durham (while here, a family of rats moved into my cell and I used to feed and play with them, it helped to pass the time a bit), Long Lartin, Bristol, Birmingham, Winchester, Wandsworth, Frankland, Parkhurst. I had more fucking drops offs than a tube train – and this was all in one year! On and on it went, one seg unit to another, one strong box to another, one beating after another. A nightmarish merry-go-round that I couldn't get off. I took hostages, got on rooftops, beat up screws, governors and other prisoners and, I have to admit, I even went a little bit mad. I'd think nothing of stripping off naked and demanding a beat down, often oiling my body up so the screws couldn't get a proper grip of me. I'd run riot round the prison if I ever got a day of freedom from the block. One time I stripped off completely, grabbed a broomstick and put a smashed bottle on one end of it, then ran around, screaming, with my makeshift spear held aloft. I knew I was nearing the edge as far as my sanity went.

It went on like this until late 1994, in fact, when I ended up back in Wakefield, down their block and into their strong box. It was here that I met a prison officer that would change my life – and my name as it happened. Mr Mick O'Hagan, a salt of the earth officer in my opinion, actually believed in me.

Despite all I'd done, all that he knew I'd done, he wanted to try to make things a little bit better for me. He disregarded anything I said about the system being unable to break me, he could see I was broken. Of course I was broken, just not beaten, yet. Mr O'Hagan was to alter my perception of everything. There are definitely some decent screws and, because they are few and far between, they remain memorable. If only all the screws were like O'Hagan and a few other good men, I'm absolutely sure that prisons would be far less dangerous places to be.

CHAPTER TWENTY-FIVE

IRENE

AT THE age of 29, my Mike was visiting his Dad, my Mick, regularly, and though I'd promised Mike I would never stand in his way of rekindling their relationship and I was fine with it, I was far from fine in reality.

My OCD was back with a vengeance, I was up and down like a bloody yo-yo again, counting and touching everything I was compelled to and my nerves were always on edge. Each time Mike set off on a visit, I would almost wear out the carpet with my pacing. It was awful, I couldn't settle until he was back home. It was the fear of the unknown, really. I didn't want to be a part of any of it, but it was all the wondering what might be going on that I struggled with.

'You look dreadful, Mum,' he said one day after he got back. 'Are you alright?'

'No, I'm not, Mike,' I said. 'I'm on bloody pins every

time you go to see your Dad, hoping it all goes well, hoping he doesn't upset you in any way, and praying to God that you're alright. Then you come back here, and never say a bloody word about it!'

'But, Mum,' Mike said, staring at me in astonishment. 'Right from the start you said you didn't want to hear about it, told me it was between me and him, and you didn't want to get involved! I stay quiet because I assume it's what you want.'

He was right, I had said that, and had said it a few times. But if I was being honest with myself, I had half-expected he might argue with me about it and insist on telling me. He never even said that he'd had a good time, or anything for that matter.

'Well, yes I did,' I said. 'But you know what I'm like, I might say all this stuff, but you know how nosey I am, I want to know, Mike. As it is, I'm not sure if it's making you happy, or what?'

Mike laughed, 'I am happy, Mum, really happy that I'm seeing my Dad, and we get along great. I see a lot of myself in him and I promise, you have nothing to worry about.'

'Okay then,' I said. 'But what do you talk about?'

'Oh my God, Mother,' Mike said, laughing out loud. 'Do we talk about you? Is that what you mean? If it is, then yes, we do, we always talk about you. Half the bloody visits are all about you, to be honest. In fact, today he gave me a message for you.'

I stared at Mike who had now picked up my crossword puzzle book and was staring at it with interest.

'Jesus Christ, Mike!' I said. 'It's like pulling bloody teeth. You can't just say something like that and then stop! What was the message?'

He teased me a bit longer and then relented.

'He said he's never forgotten you, Mum. There's not a day gone by, in all these years, when he hasn't thought about you, and me. He actually talks like he's still in love with you, Mum. It's mad.'

The strangest thing happened to me at that moment, something that hadn't happened in donkey's years, I got butterflies in my stomach. My heart did a crazy flip and I felt my cheeks redden too. Honestly, it was like I was 17 years old again.

'Cheeky sod,' I said, trying not to giggle. 'Why is that mad? What's not to love, eh?'

From that day on, I lived for the times that Mike would go on a visit and then come home passing messages on to me, telling me all about the time he'd spent with his Dad. I would get excited watching for him coming down the path and would almost fall over myself to get to the door and let him in. I'd always have Mike's favourite teas ready for the occasion, so we could sit together for a bit while I listened to what he had to say.

'Why don't you just write to him, Mum,' Mike said one day. 'You know you want to, and it would save me having to remember everything you both have to say to each other. Honestly, it's like being back in school, passing on love notes for your mates, it's ridiculous!'

He passed me one of his own prison letters, one that he'd received from his Dad, to show me the address and prison number, and that was the first time I realised Mick was using the name Charles Bronson on all of his communication. The handwriting, as ever, was unmistakable and, just like it did years before, the sight of it took my breath away.

'Well,' I huffed. 'If I do ever decide to write him, I certainly won't be calling him bloody Charles, or Charlie, and that's a promise. Charles bloody Bronson, what on earth was he thinking?'

Mike laughed, but I meant it. He was Mick to me and always would be, I could never imagine him as Charlie and I never would. I folded up the piece of paper Mike had handed me and put it in a kitchen drawer. I wasn't ready to write just yet, I'd lived a whole lifetime without him being in it, had two more children, both grown up, and had two more failed relationships. What could I say these days? We had nothing in common other than our Mike, and he was a man now. It wasn't like I could update Mick on his progress or anything, he led his own life and I wasn't that big a part of it any more.

A couple of years later, after a particularly nice dream about Mick, I picked up a pen and paper and I wrote a letter to him. I found as I wrote that I couldn't stop, it went on and on. *I hope he's an avid bloody reader*, I thought as I popped it across the counter at the post office. I think that first letter went on for about six pages. I talked about anything and everything – the family, the kids, my Mum and Dad, his Mum and Dad.

I wrote about funny memories I had of us as a couple and the people we used to meet, the places we went to. I found it really therapeutic, actually, to revisit the past like this, as a lot of those memories had been buried away for years, so I felt as if a weight had been lifted from me when I posted it.

The letters from Mick came thick and fast after that, and we were communicating regularly like this for years. Pretty soon, we knew everything about each other again and it was like we'd never been apart.

He changed his name yet again, this time to Charles Salvador in respect to the artist he so admired, or so I thought. I learned years later that Salvador, when translated, meant somebody who helped sinners, and was a name for a man of peace. Whatever the reason, I still refused to call him anything other than Mick.

He would tell me how much I meant to him, and how my letters were changing him for the better, calming him down and giving him hope for the future. I didn't know what all this meant, but I knew I couldn't and shouldn't stop. I realised that I needed these letters just as much as my ex-husband did and it felt like I'd got my Mick back, even if it was at a distance.

Please let me phone you, Irene, Mick would plead in letter after letter, *I know you're scared, baby, but I need to hear your voice, my beautiful Princess. I've never forgotten how you sound, you know. That nervous giggle and that laugh of yours, I'd love to hear it again, even if it's just once. All you have to do is phone the prison and add your number to my call list, that's it.*

But it was 2012 before I plucked up the courage to do that, and I was so nervous for that first call. The governor had told me it could take a week for it all to be checked and approved, so when it came just three days later, I wasn't expecting it.

'Irene,' the unmistakeable, gravelly, cockney voice said, sending my heart fluttering almost out of my mouth. 'It's me, your Mick, how you doing, Princess?'

Oh my God, I was overwhelmed with all kinds of emotions, happiness, regret, sadness, and yes, a yearning to reach out and touch Mick through the phone. It was madness after all these years, but there it was. I still loved the man. I could admit that to myself now, but not to anybody else, not yet.

The phone calls continued regularly after that, right up to the present day, and I still get butterflies when I see the prison number pop up on the screen because, of course, we all have mobile phones now. I was devastated when his parole hearing in 2023 didn't go in our favour because now Mick has spent 53 years behind bars. That's not a typo, that's 53 years, and it all started with a seven-year sentence. Mick and I are both 73 years old now, but I don't consider myself old and neither does Mick. We have been suspended in time, each waiting for the other without realising it, so that our life can continue, and only then will we allow ourselves to grow old gracefully. I pray with every fibre of my body that this next hearing in 2025 will see a parole board who will show some mercy and acknowledge that Mick is no longer a danger to anybody. The danger these days is more towards him, than from him, and he simply wants to live out whatever years he has left with dignity and in peace.

CHAPTER TWENTY-EIGHT

MICK

AS SOON as I arrived at Wakefield, I was dragged off to the strong box, the concrete coffin, the cage, hell on earth. A place where I expected to be brutalised and subjected to the most horrific cruelty by the worst screws I'd met in this country, and I prepared myself, mentally, for a few months for this type of torture.

It never happened though.

I waited for days for it to start. The box was bad enough, but the torture was usually the worst part. This time there was a new officer I'd only come across a couple of times. He was on the wing the last time I was here, but now he worked this block. Mr Mick O'Hagan. After not speaking for a few days, probably waiting for me to calm down, he opened the hatch one morning to speak to me.

'Charlie, can we have a chat, mate?' He called. 'I'd like to speak with you for a bit if I can.'

'What is it?' I asked, having to shout due to the two steel doors, designed so we could barely hear anything outside of the box.

'Don't you get sick of this, Charlie?' He asked. 'You do know they'll never let you out if you continue like this. I just don't understand it, mate.'

I squished up to the inner door in silence as I listened.

'You should do something constructive while you're in there, Charlie,' he went on. 'Something you can feel proud of yourself about. Still do your exercise routines, but surely there's more you want?'

'In here?' I asked. 'What the fuck can I do in here?'

'Yes, in there,' Mr O'Hagan shouted back. 'That box is only like any other cell, Charlie, there's loads of stuff you could do. Write, look back on your life and write about it, draw, paint, make cartoons, anything, you can easily do any of that in there. Read a book, study something, there's all sorts you can do.'

I laughed and started to do my press ups, but I did allow myself to ponder on it. It actually might lift my spirits, I thought, and give me something to do to pass the time.

The next morning, the hatch opened and Mr O'Hagan passed me some paper, a book, some pencils and coloured pens. I stared at them for a moment, then said, 'Thanks, me old china, I'll have a go.'

That was the start of me becoming Charles Salvador, if the truth be known, but I didn't make that change just yet.

I practiced, I experimented, I wrote poetry. I spent five months in that cage, drawing and writing poems every single day for as long as I could. Mr O'Hagan was very proud. I'd show him almost every day what I'd done and he'd tell me how good it was. I had so much respect for him, for the way he treated me, he was a proper man, a man's man, and he didn't have a cruel bone in his body. He taught me that just as there are good and bad cons, the same went for prison officers, we just had to give each other a chance.

After I got out of there, I continued my hobby, experimenting with paint and other mediums and I really let loose with my imagination. I drew or painted whatever was in my head. Some of it was funny, but some of it was dark, deep and dangerous too. It didn't matter, it was my way of expressing myself and I'd never been happier.

I still had my moments, even though I was now back in touch with my beautiful Irene and my son, Mike. I had beautiful things in my life now, my art and my family, but my reputation within the system had grown organically and had a life of its own. A new breed of gangsters had taken over the population while I'd spent a lifetime in solitary, and a lot of them wanted to be 'the one' who took out Charles Bronson.

I found myself having to be on the defence every minute of every day. It was fucking horrendous. How was I meant to keep on the straight and narrow and prove to my family that I had changed, when every fucker was trying to off me behind the wall?

I took hostages for protection at times, and other times to make demands that I be moved or treated to better conditions. I had to engage in fights, I had no choice. Two men once came up behind me and started stabbing me. They wanted me dead and made it clear. I would never name them, however, and denied it happened. Despite what they did to me, I couldn't ever be a grass.

I did lose my marbles when my Dad died, I admit that, and that was when I took the Iraqi hostages, three of them. One of them had barged into me a week earlier and never said sorry. While I was feeling really bad about my Dad, I remembered he'd done that, and got angry about his ignorance and disrespect, so I took him and two of his mates to my cell and kept them there. To be fair, I was a lunatic that day, and had no agenda and no reason for it other than I was upset about my Dad.

Shit, I was bad that day, I was singing like a mad man and they were terrified of me. I made them tickle my feet and call me general and I hit one of them over the head with a metal tray. I did feel bad about that though, because it brought tears to his eyes, and so I picked the tray back up, handed it to him and insisted that he hit my head with it as hard as he could. Bless him, he couldn't bring himself to do it hard and I'd really hurt him, so I told him to do it another three times and then we'd call it quits. I think I demanded a helicopter and a few other ludicrous things in exchange for their freedom, but in the end, I agreed to end it peacefully that day. I allowed the hostages to go free, but asked that I be allowed to walk to segregation without being strapped up. Unbelievably, the governor agreed. I had to go to the visiting court for that and got seven more years added to my sentence, but my solicitor appealed it and got it reduced to five. Still a bastard of a sentence though.

I took a couple more hostages for various reasons over the next few years, the most serious of which was an art teacher called Phil. He had said something off about some of my artwork and I took offence to it. I was livid and kept him for almost two days, treating him appallingly if I'm honest, I was like a full-on fucking lunatic. I even electrocuted myself and went unconscious for a minute or so when I ripped a washing machine off the wall in a fit of temper. It was bad, and I caused a ton of damage to the art room. I was pissed off afterwards because I was proud of art and had won no less than five Koestler awards for my personal work. It was a shame really that it was an art teacher who sent me over the edge that day. I admitted it and got a discretionary life sentence for it, to serve a minimum of three years.

What they did to me next was really unexpected, and most unwelcome.

In 1999, the prison service, in their infinite wisdom,

decided that there were three prisoners in Great Britain who could not be contained by the normal structure of a prison and its segregation blocks. They were deemed too dangerous to be allowed anywhere near staff or prisoners at any time and that they posed a high risk if they were ever to be in contact with any other person. To counter this, it was announced that a special prison unit had been built especially to house these prisoners, at Woodhill Jail. One of those prisoners was me, and I was transferred there immediately. It was all over the papers and the prison service stated, 'This doesn't mean these men will be left to rot, and no longer be able to be rehabilitated. We are not throwing away the key, all we are saying is that these men will go through the system in a different, more appropriate way.' When asked what form that would take, the representative said, 'We aren't sure at the moment, but we are working on it.' Yes, right!

The other two prisoners who were being housed in the unit were serial killer Robert Maudsley, nicknamed Hannibal the Cannibal after the psychopath in the movie, *Silence of the Lambs*. He'd fucking garrotted his own uncle! The other guest, Reginald Wilson, was a diagnosed psychopath who had murdered a doctor in his own home and then bragged about it to the police. Both murderers, both mad as fuck, and both would kill their own mothers if given the chance. Me? I was an armed robber at best – a prison activist and hostage-taker (only in prison, by the way) at worst. Yet here I was, lumped in with the two of them. Okay, so yes, I had been a violent fucker at times and bashed a few skulls when the situation called for it, but even so, I wouldn't have said I was anywhere near on par with the cannibal and the psycho! And they say I'm mental! The prison service ought to look in a fucking mirror.

Mark Leech, editor of the Prisons' Handbook, knew what he was talking about, if the rest of 'em didn't, he said, 'The clear lesson of the last 20 years is that creating increasingly strict regimes for such prisoners does not decrease the danger they represent to others. On the contrary, it clearly increases it.' Why can't they listen to that man?

The special cages we were housed in are unlike any other I've seen. Bars, mesh, unbreakable glass and cameras, so we can be seen at all times, and all the furniture is made out of compressed cardboard that can't be used as a weapon and can't be burned. You'd think I might have built up a relationship with the other blokes I was down there with, but I was next door to Bob, that's Maudsley, and I fell out with him big-style. I tried to be alright with him, even though I could clearly see what a fucking nutcase he was. I gave him a watch as a gift. I then heard him give it to one of the screws and he told him to throw it away as he didn't want it. I shouted to him that he was a disrespectful fucker and that I'd had it with him. He shouted back that he'd take my eyes out and eat my heart. Mad bastard! That makes us mortal enemies in my book and I never spoke to the ungrateful fucker again.

In 2014, I changed my name by deed poll to Charles Salvador and I once again put everything I had into my artwork and poetry. I continued to win awards and my work often sold for big money which I donated a lot of to charities. My last jam role (parole hearing) was in 2023 and I felt sure I had every chance of release. I'd been a model prisoner for a long time, and I made it clear that I was no threat to anybody anymore. They knocked me back and I was devastated. The top and bottom of it is this: the parole board say that because I've been in solitary confinement, there is no evidence that I am not a danger to others because that hasn't been tested for years. The prison system says that I must remain in solitary for my own protection now, and because they also can't say how much of a risk I'd be to others without testing the idea, and they won't do this, just in case.

Well, fucking hell, where does that leave me then?

EPILOGUE

CHARLES SALVADOR AND IRENE DUNROE
TO JULIE SHAW

We the willing, led by the unknowing,
Have been doing the impossible, for the ungrateful
For so long, with so little,
Are we now qualified, to do anything,
With nothing at all.

I love that quote, said Charles, on a postcard to me one day.
*I think it's very powerful, and was told to me by a prisoner I became
very good friends with, Andy Doughall, God rest his soul, he died in
prison years ago, but was banged up with me in Parkhurst in the 80s.
I've never forgotten either him or that quote.*

To me, it could relate to any prisoner who has spent
years in solitary, expected to follow a regime we don't
agree with, under the orders of a system we believe is
wrong, and yet somehow, despite everything, we find a
way to survive.

The quote is attributed by some to Mother Teresa, and

I found it strange that Charles would have such a strong reaction to it, but after I really thought about it, I could completely see his reasoning. Charles wrote me many, many letters and sent lots of emails and we built up a really good relationship. When he realised that I wanted to write this book, not glamourising his crimes and not raging against the system, but getting deep into his heart and soul and trying to discover what made him tick, his letters changed from the usual jailhouse tales, to pouring his heart out about love and loss. I began to see a direct correlation between his life behind bars and Irene's life on the outside.

He recalls the women he'd previously married and why he divorced them, and then he talks in a reflective way about what all these years in institutions have done to him and how desperately he wants to be released. He talks about his love for Irene and how, even now, as a woman in her 70s, she makes his heart flutter whenever he sees her.

He pleads for a peaceful life, one in which there are no young criminals and gangsters wanting to make a name for themselves by trying to kill him, one where he isn't constantly looking over his shoulder for a young prison officer looking for retribution from some old feud.

This Charles Salvador doesn't seem to be a monster. He knows he can never take back the things he's done, but asks, 'Isn't 58 years enough? 58 years of being treated less than human, being beaten, being tortured. I'm an old man now, and yes, facing society will be hard, the system has made sure of that, but can't I have the chance in my final years to lie in my own bed, to breathe in fresh air, to have some peace of mind and shake off the horrors of prison?'

Irene adds to this plea and states that enough is enough. 'I believe fate has always kept us together in some way,' she says, 'and I believe that Mick and I have one last fight in us and, much like all our fights, we should be there for each other. If the parole board finally shows some mercy and agrees, I don't know what that might look like for us, I really don't, but the universe always has a plan, so let's just wait and see.'

Irene also told me that after she divorced Dave, she spent a few years with another man, whom she moved in with for a time. Unfortunately, he died a few years later, but she'd shared some happy times with him. It was during that time that she started to work for Ann Summers, the famous lingerie company and she has stayed working for them. Even now, in her 70s, Irene can be found helping customers to select their sex toys and sexy lingerie.

On another postcard, Charles wrote, *A man's first true love is wonderful, unique, special. It is absolute, beautiful, priceless and it lasts a lifetime. You can have a thousand lovers, a million friends, but that first love can never be replaced. Irene was the 'special one' and I was blessed to have her in my life. I am one lucky bastard!* He followed this up with a letter, again stating how much Irene meant and still means to him now. He ended it by asking, with a drawing of a winking face, 'The million dollar question is, will Irene and me get married again when I get released? Watch this space, and tell *OK!* magazine they can do the photos if they pay us the exclusive rights! Why not, Julie? Irene deserves a happy ending.'

When I asked Charles what his biggest regret is, he left me a voicemail, as well as sending the reply in a letter.

'I have no regrets, Julie,' he said. 'My actions have cost me half a century of my fucked-up life, but what a journey it has been. I go to sleep with a smile on my face and I wake up happy. My greatest achievement in life is my son, Michael, who is 53 years old now, and we've not ever had a pint together, one of my dreams is that. A son is priceless because he will go on when I am dust. He will continue the journey with my eyes. Sure, it's sad, our years of separation, and yes, I've missed out on being there for him, but my love is strong, till the end of time.

'I'm a very lucky man, I'm blessed with my Irene and Mike and my good friends. Loyal, honourable and respectful, they are true family to me and I love them all. Sadly, a lot of them have passed on, but I truly miss them, especially the Kray twins. They were so good to me and were definitely not like today's plastic gangsters!'

He ended that letter with reference to his upcoming parole, set for May 2025. 'I'm hoping this next jam role will finally see me freed and, if not, they need to say why not! And then justify it! It's time, Julie, why do they keep lingering it on? What sense is there keeping me locked away, how am I a danger to society? They let out murderers, rapists, paedophiles every day, they are the danger! I've never been more ready to come out. It's fate, please, let them open those gates and let me fly.'

As I write, Charles has arranged for me to go visit him in a couple of weeks, in Long Lartin prison where he is now being held – that is of course if they don't move him before then, that's never off the cards for Charles, and I've organised for Irene to go on the visit with me. We are both very much looking forward to it. I speak to Irene all the time on the phone and she giggles all the time if we talk about how much 'her Mick' (she won't call him Charles) still obviously loves her.

'I'm in my 70s now, Julie,' she says. 'It's a bit late for all that stuff, don't you think?'

'I pray every night that Mick gets his parole, and finds his peace. I want that for him, I really do. We both need this. I know Mick says he's been happy, but I want him to truly experience real happiness out here, not in that place. He doesn't deserve to still be there.'

I shed a tear myself one night when I received an unexpected voice message from Charles that he wanted me to pass on to Irene. Maybe they were words he didn't feel able to say directly to her, but he wanted her to hear them: 'Irene, surprise! I love you Princess, I always have, always will. Your beautiful eyes could melt butter, just by looking at it. You're a wonderful woman, Irene, that I've had the privilege of having in my life and please don't ever forget that. Do you remember that time you came to visit me years ago, when Michael was just a baby? You looked me straight in the eye and you said, (puts on a female voice) 'you, Mick, are gonna end up in the loony bin, the nuthouse, if you carry on!' I told you to give it a rest, but you were right, Princess, you always was. You make my life worth living, Irene, you are the type of wonderful person that can brighten up anyone's day, you really are, and I truly love you. Keep smiling, Princess, because when you smile my darling, you make the whole world smile. Adios amigos, see ya, senorita! Mick.

I sent the lovely message straight to Irene and she rang me back as soon as she'd listened to it.

'Oh, Julie,' she said. 'How sweet was that? He's a hopeless romantic you know, always has been. I loved that, thank you so much, and just tell Mick that I said – bless him.'

AUTHOR OVERVIEW

INTRODUCTION

This report outlines the current progress, challenges, and next steps for Charles, who has been undergoing therapy while serving an extraordinarily lengthy sentence in prison. Originally sentenced for armed robbery in the 1970s, Charles's journey through the penal system has been marked by significant struggles and remarkable resilience.

PROGRESS HIGHLIGHTS

Charles has shown considerable growth. He has actively engaged in discussions about his past, demonstrating insight into how his experiences have shaped his worldview. His art has blossomed; not only has he developed a unique style, but he has also channelled his emotions into his paintings, which have gained recognition and offered financial support for children's charities. This shift from a life defined by violence to one of creativity and philanthropy reflects a significant change in his mindset.

Additionally, Charles has expressed a deep desire for reconciliation with his past actions and the people he may have hurt. He has shown a willingness to explore the impact of his long-term solitary confinement on his mental health and interpersonal relationships. His commitment to personal growth has been commendable, and he has begun to envision a future beyond prison walls. Through letters and other methods of communication Charles has connected with a series of new friends who are upstanding citizens, all of whom have expressed a desire to help him along his journey towards freedom. These same friends have assured Charles that they will be there to help in the event he is released.

CHALLENGES

Despite these positive strides, Charles faces considerable challenges as he approaches his next parole hearing. The prison system has maintained strict controls and has not facilitated opportunities for Charles to interact with other inmates in a more normal environment. This lack of exposure to communal living raises concerns for the parole board, as it weighs the potential risks of his release.

His history of violence, seemingly in part a response to the brutal conditions he endured, continues to haunt his prospects for freedom. The prison administration has been reluctant to test his current behaviour in a less restrictive setting, which further complicates his case. These systemic barriers to rehabilitation and reintegration into society remain significant obstacles for him.

NEXT STEPS

As we approach the upcoming parole hearing, it will be crucial to advocate for Charles' right to demonstrate his progress in a more open environment. Suggestions include:

Requesting a Reassessment of Placement: Propose that Charles be temporarily placed in a less restrictive wing or participate in structured group therapy sessions to provide evidence of his ability to coexist peacefully with others.

Art Therapy Programs: Encourage the establishment of art therapy programs that allow Charles to engage with other inmates while expressing himself creatively. This could help build social skills and demonstrate his commitment to non-violence.

Continued Therapy: Ongoing individual therapy sessions should focus on coping strategies, emotional regulation, and conflict resolution to further prepare Charles for potential reintegration into society.

Support Network: Establishing a support network of

advocates, including former inmates who have success-
fully reintegrated, may help to bolster Charles' case and
provide a broader context of rehabilitation.

CONCLUSION

For those who have found themselves victims of Charles'
violence over the years, the 'why' is perhaps not so
important as the impact on them and their lives. And the
idea that some – perhaps many – think he should never
see the light of day again is perhaps understandable.

But for Charles, his personal journey is a testament to
resilience and the potential – even if not always realised
– for change, even in the most challenging circumstances.
As he prepares for his next parole hearing, his team will
want to highlight his progress and advocate for opportunities that can demonstrate his readiness for reintegration.
The road ahead may be fraught with challenges, but with
continued support and understanding, there is hope for
him to finally achieve the peace he says he seeks in the
twilight of his life.

So, can a long-term prisoner truly be considered rehabilitated, and if not, why not? The Prison Reform Trust
suggests that the prisoners they spoke to, those serving ten
years or more, were at a loss regarding what was expected
of them in order to meet the expectations of any future
parole board. They found that prisoners were confused

and disillusioned by the apparently simple proposition that they are required to reduce 'risk'. While talk of risk pervades prison life and affects many aspects of prisoners' experiences, this catch-all term masks important details – risk of what, from what, to whom, in what circumstances?

Demonstrating reduced risk is of particular importance to those whose release ultimately depends upon approval by the Parole Board – and if recent proposals become law – the Secretary of State for Justice.

The report suggests that this confusion stems from a mismatch between what prisons appear to expect from prisoners – broadly, compliance with the rules – and what those in probation and the Parole Board are looking for prisoners to demonstrate to secure their own development and eventual release.

The report recommends that HM Prison and Probation Service should develop a long-term prisoner policy framework. It should equip staff working with long-term prisoners to assess risk; communicate this effectively with prisoners and other criminal justice professionals; and give explicit guidance and direction on what kinds of behaviour may demonstrate lowered and elevated risk in future assessments.

It also recommends earlier involvement with the Parole Board in reviewing progress. This would allow any potential roadblocks to release to be identified and a plan to be developed which would outline the steps prisoners can take. With so many years in custody to work with, the system should be aiming for far more prisoners to be ready and safe for release when the period set for punishment expires.

The trouble for Charles is that he doesn't fit neatly into any category. He has already served more than 20 years over his life tariff and, in the last few years, hasn't reoffended, certainly since his last parole hearing, so why is he still inside?

This book started with Charles posing the question: are we a product of our environment? After all my research and interviews with Charles, and after completing this book, the answer remains unclear. For sure, our environment helps to shape us because we have to adapt in order to survive, but does that then take away our responsibility to ensure we behave in a suitable manner? It does not. The real questions we should be asking, in my opinion, are: Can a person truly be rehabilitated? Does our justice system always ensure that the punishment fits the crime? Do our prisons give prisoners the opportunities to enable them to live safely back in society?

Charles once said of Irene in a letter to me: 'I will miss my Irene till the day I die.'

EPILOGUE

PEOPLE KEPT asking me if I was nervous prior to the visit, but I wasn't, I didn't have any reason to be. After all, I had already built up a relationship with both Charles and Irene during the previous six months or so, through phone calls, letters and messages. Through writing such personal accounts of their lives in the book, I felt I knew them quite well. The reality however, of visiting a maximum security prison, taught me that I did have reason to be nervous.

I met with Irene first, at a local hotel, where we caught up for a while and had a drink, and the first thing that struck me was how young she looked. I couldn't believe she was 72 years old – the same age as Charles – when I saw her waiting at a table for me. Long, shiny black hair, perfectly applied make-up, and she was wearing black leather skinny jeans, a black off the shoulder top and a trendy fur jacket, topped off with high heeled black boots. She was slim and tiny at five feet tall with a lovely, welcoming smile. Irene giggles a lot too, and this adds to her charm and the illusion of her being at least 20 years younger. We were both tiny, with long black hair, and we wore the same clothes, it was mad. Irene noticed it too and joked that we could be long lost sisters

At first sight, from the visitor's car park, Long Lartin Maximum Security Prison looked quite unimposing. It had a modern look to it and the visitor's centre, where we had to sit and wait after booking in, was warm, colourful and quite comfortable. As it was half term, I noticed there were quite a few wives and children waiting to visit their loved ones, and there was a large play area to one side for the kids. At that point, Irene and I had to fill in what we wanted to order from the canteen. A list of food, drinks and lots of chocolates were on offer, but Irene was a little upset because Charles had asked that as well as cups of tea, could she get him a ham roll, and there were no sandwiches at all on offer that day. We settled for various chocolate bars, crisps and biscuits and were told that they would be delivered to us once we were in our actual visit.

When our number was called, we were led through to various different areas where we were scanned, body searched and had our fingerprints taken, as well as having to be searched by a sniffer dog – in case we were taking drugs inside! The fingerprint process had to be done in three more areas and then finally we were photographed before being taken to where we would meet Charles, flanked by two prison guards. They explained to us that we would have to pass through the regular visiting hall where other prisoners shared their visits, but Charles would be in a locked, solitary room as he wasn't allowed to mix. All of this process made me nervous, driving home the point that even a maximum security prison had to make special arrangements for this particular prisoner.

Finally, after all of that, and with Irene clinging to my arm to steady herself as she was really scared of the whole process, we reached a double locked door, behind which we were told Charles would be waiting for us. Our two guards unlocked it and stood back, indicating for us to go inside. I don't know what I was expecting as I'd read on the internet that one visitor had gone to see Charles and had to sit outside a caged cell to chat with him, but I was pleasantly surprised.

He was sitting on a large blue, comfortable chair in front of a coffee table, and there was a sofa opposite him. This was in a large, colourful room, decorated with art works, flowers and more sofas with cushions. When he saw us, he leapt up and held out his arms, "Irene, my Irene!' he said, 'and Julie! Wow! You look like fucking sisters, come 'ere and give us a hug, girls.'

Irene rushed forward for her hug and I could see that

she had tears in her eyes. I also hugged him then and sat down. I allowed the two of them to catch up – after all it had been a year or so since Irene had last seen Charles face to face. As I sat and listened, it struck me that Charles also looked incredibly young for his age. He was the biggest man I had ever seen, he was just massive! Tall, broad and very, very muscular, he dwarfed not just me and Irene but also the two prison officers who were sitting in a corner of the room to supervise the visit. I couldn't help staring at his face. I could clearly see that he didn't have one line or wrinkle on it anywhere! His arms, exposed as he was wearing a T-shirt, looked like the arms of a much younger man – they were also huge. If I didn't know any better, and someone had asked me to guess his age, I would have definitely said 50 tops. A strange thought occurred to me in that moment as I watched Irene and Charles, it was as if time had stood still for them both. Like some higher power had decided at some point that they shouldn't age, not until they were both free to be together again. People later said to me that no wonder he looks young, he hasn't been exposed to the elements or had any stress about day to day life – bills, the cost of living etc, and has probably always had a good diet. But then how does that explain that Irene hasn't aged either?

They spent the next two and a half hours laughing, sharing stories and talking about all kinds of things. Charles was a gracious host to me too, always asking questions about my family, my writing and, as he'd read lots of excerpts from the new book, he couldn't quite get over how I'd managed to capture his 'voice' so well.

'I read one page,' he said, 'then I read it again, and I would swear that I'd fucking written it myself! I couldn't get my 'ead around it, Jue, it was like you was in my fucking skull!'

I explained that as a writer, it was my job to do this, but it was funny to see him so bewildered by it. We had our tea and snacks delivered and then sat back and listened as Charles regaled us with funny prison stories about some of the characters he'd met over the years. He also spoke seriously about his upcoming parole, and then he dropped a bombshell. Prisoners, by law, are entitled to a review – parole hearing – every two years so, by rights, Charles's had been set for March. We already knew that it had been put back – due to a backlog, apparently – until May. That was bad enough for him, but the night before, he'd been told matter of factly that it would now be the end of the year. That would be almost three years since his last hearing. Charles sighed, 'It is what it is,' he said, 'and I will deal with it. They assume I'm going to kick off about it, and then they have something to hold me inside with at the jam roll (parole), but that's not me anymore, Jue, I just smile and tell them it's fine. I can't do a thing about it, can I? So why kick off? I'm not giving 'em what they want, not at this stage in my life. I'm not a fighter anymore, I'm an artist, a reformed activist, a different man. I'm 72 for fuck's sake, I'm not gonna start beating guards up again, not at my age.'

I looked at him and saw how serious he was, but I also thought, this man could very easily beat up six or seven men if he wanted to, despite his age. The fact that he must know this, and yet choose not to, said a lot about his resilience and determination to reach his freedom. To cheer us all up, Irene said, 'Tell Julie about the first thing you're going to do when you get out, Mick.'

Charles laughed and threw out his arms to the sides and looked up towards the ceiling, 'I'm gonna find a beach,' he said, without looking down, 'kick off my shoes to feel the sand between my fucking toes, smile at the sun, and then sing "What a Wonderful World".'

He actually sang the whole song all the way through (think a younger version of Uncle Albert from *Only Fools and Horses* for voice). At the end, Irene and I started to clap. When the visit had to come to an end I felt somehow a little sad. Six guards entered to escort Charles back to his isolation cell and I could see that Charles was a little upset too when he hugged Irene and she had tears in her eyes. 'What do you think, Irene,' he asked, looking into her eyes. 'Me and you, when I get out, shall we re-marry?'

'Could I put up with you, Mick, for the rest of my life?' she asked, jokingly. 'Let me think about it.'

'You do that,' he said as he kissed her lips gently, 'because I'm coming home, Irene, I can feel it, Princess.'

He then gave me a hug and a peck on the cheek and told me he hoped I'd visit again.

'But I don't want you coming all this way, Jue,' he said, referring to the four-hour drive, 'hopefully when they next move me – which they will, they always do, I might be a bit closer to you. That'll be better for you.'

Irene cried a little as we watched him being led off, flanked by the six officers, and we were both a lot quieter on our journey back home that day, each lost in our own thoughts.

ACKNOWLEDGEMENTS

I'D LOVE to thank my wonderful agent, Andrew Lownie, for encouraging me, and for always having my back. You really do make me want to always do my best, Andrew, I can't thank you enough!

And to the whole team at Mirror Books. Thanks to Clare Fitzsimons and Christine Costello on the editorial team, Claire Brown in marketing and Chris Collins who designed the cover. Thank you so much for believing in me and helping me every step of the way. Huge appreciation to both Irene and Charlie for the late night calls, the endless messages and the wonderful, long letters. We've had lots of chuckles along the way and you've both made it so fun. Friends for life now guys!

Finally, thanks as always, must go to my wonderful family for putting up with me when I'm 'on a roll'. I couldn't do what I do without your support, especially my hubby, Ben and my mum and dad, Keith and Shirley, who always think everything I do is just brilliant.

Top left: Irene as a child

Top right: Irene and Mick as a young couple

Left: Family photo featuring Irene (*far left*), Mick (*second from right*) and their son Mike

Top left: Mick leaving prison in 1987

Top right: Irene and Mick holding Mike as a baby

Right: Mick and Irene in their younger years

Below: Irene holding Mike as a baby

Mike and his father pictured in 2010

Postcard sent to Irene from prison, date unknown

A photo sent to Irene from Mick in prison in 1987

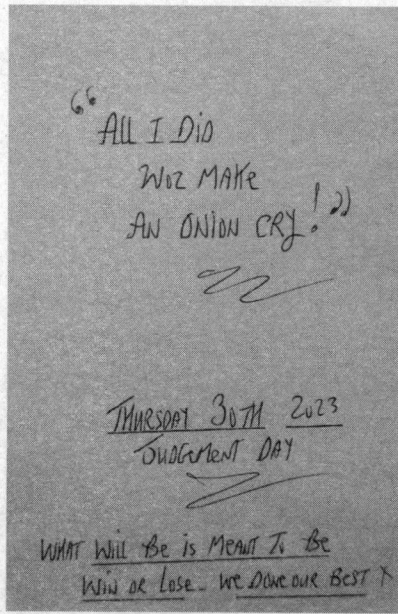

Various writings from Mick to Irene from prison between 2022 and 2023

Roy "Mean Machine" Shaw, professional boxer and former Cat A prisoner with Mick

Charles Bronson stages a protest on the roof of Broadmoor Hospital. June 20, 1983.

Kray Twins Ronald and Reginald, friends of Charles in prison, pictured here in 1966

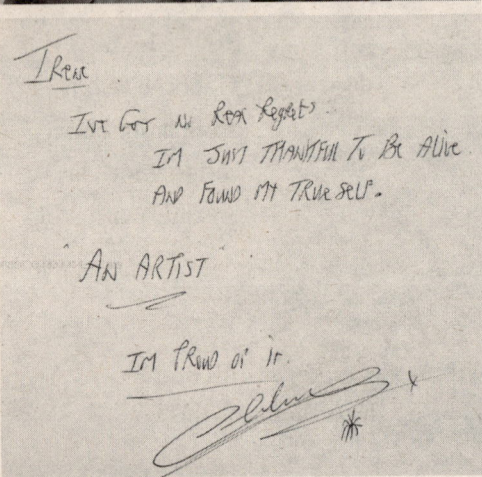

"Irene, I've got no real regrets. I'm just thankful to be alive. And found my true self. An Artist – I'm proud of it."

Letter from Mick to Irene from prison

Salvador 1314 Seguoin. Martin

Jullo

Xmas 1974. No 1 Record (it will Be Lonely this Xmas)
I was stood on a table looking through the Bars watching the
Snow fall at Walton. I feel Sad.
Our 1st Xmas separate unknown our Last too.
We would have a couple of visits in 1975. We were Gradually
Becoming strangers. it was tough for Irene as a single Mother
For Me it was such a journey of Madness
Without Irene I was lost and empty

The Special thing about Irene was she was so
Unique. a one off. Priceless
Very Dizzy. Funny. Loving. Kind. She Made Me laugh alot.
She Made Me feel so Magical.
But a guy like Me could never Be really what a Normal
Husband could or should Be.
I was Born for Action. Danger and unpredictability
I get bored with life so easily
And that when the saying come into it
You Don't Know what you got
Till you lose it.
Then it smashes everything to Pieces
All the Dreams Become Nightmares. It Become a lifetime
So years later im still living this crazy life
And Irene surviving the Best she can
Funny His changed

Michaels Now 52 yo old.. Hes Not even Met
Me a Grandfather (Yet)
Always Hope..
Me a Grandad. Wow. Ill Be the Best.
Irene a Granny! So Shes Out Up on Me.
I even once she Remarried she tried so Hard
To Move on and forget me. But How could she when
Every so often I would Be on the News for some Mad

2   PROTECT. OR ACT OF VIOLENCE. MEMORIES WOULD FLOOD HER MIND
AND DON'T THEY SAY YOUR FIRST LOVE IS THE REAL LOVE
OUR LOVE WAS SO REAL. I'VE NEVER FELT SO LOVED.
I USED TO GET SAD WHEN SHE WALKED OUT OF THE ROOM
JUST TO MAKE A CUP OF TEA. OR GO OUT FOR THE DAY
I WOULD FEEL EMPTY
   FUCK ME IF THERE WOULD OF BEEN A MOBILE PHONE I WOULD OF
CALLED EVERY 5 MIN.
   I ONCE WATCHED HER GET A BUS. AND FELT SHE WAS
NEVER COMING BACK. THE BUS WOULD BLOW UP
   TO SAY I WAS OVER THE TOP WOULD BE AN UNDERSTATEMENT
   THE CUDDLES. THE HOLDING HANDS. DOING THINGS TOGETHER.
LOOKING BACK I GUESS I WAS TOTALLY IN LOVE
   BUT EVEN LOVERS NEED THERE OWN TIME. SPACE.
   YOU HAVE TO LET GO. NOT BE SO POSSESSIVE. I WAS MORE
OF A PROTECTOR, A MINDER.
I WAS SO UN GROWN UP. IMMATURE
   I WAS GREAT AT DEBT COLLECTING. CRIMINALITY. MAKING DEALS
BUT I WAS A CRAP HUSBAND
   THE REAL LIFE IS NOT A FANTASY. A DREAM, ITS A
BLOODY KICK IN THE HEAD. REALITY AT ITS BEST
   BILLS. WORRY. ANXIETIES. STRESS.
EVERYTHING A FAMILY HAVE TO STRUGGLE AND BATTLE FOR TO OVERCOME
THE ADVERSITY
   SHE HAD A PAIR OF WHITE ZIP UP BOOTS. I LOVED THEM BOOTS
WITH A SHORT WHITE DRESS. WHITE PANTIES. WHITE BRA AND
WHITE SILK SHIRT. RED LIPS. GORGEOUS BLACK HAIR THAT SMELT LIKE
ROSES. I REALLY COULD OF BEEN A TOP MODEL SHE EVEN WALKED
LIKE AN ANGEL. AND SMELT WONDERFUL
   SHE HAD THE SKIN THAT GLOWED WHEN OUT OF THE BATH
I USED TO DRY HER WITH A BIG WHITE FLUFFY TOWEL
      YEP THATS IRENE IN A NUT SHELL
ONE SEXY LOVELY BEAUTIFUL SOUL.
   IN SUFFERS IN HELL I'VE NEVER ONCE NOT THOUGHT OF HER
ILL MISS HER TILL THE DAY I DIE
                                    CRIMBI DAY
                                    2024

"The real life is not a fantasy, a dream, it's a bloody kick to the head."
Continuation of Mick's letter to Julie, sent on Christmas Day
in 2024

Mick's mother Eira holding a photo of her son

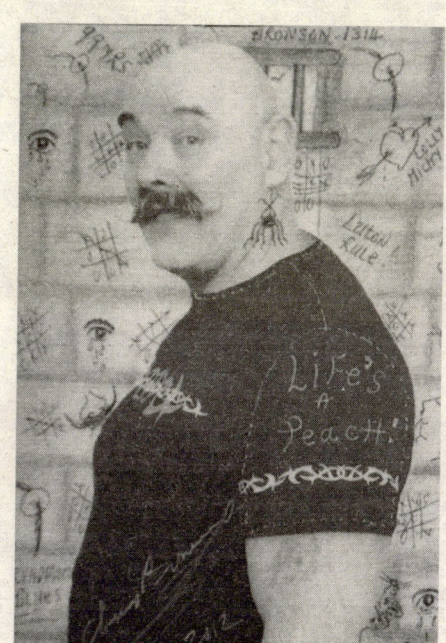

Charles Salvador, taken November 5, 2021